All Things Relationships

Kimberly Moses And Co-Authors

Copyright © 2021 by **Kimberly Moses and Co-authors**

All rights reserved. No part of this publication may be reproduced, distributed or transmitted in any form or by any means, including photocopying, recording, or other electronic or mechanical methods, without the prior written permission of the publisher, except in the case of brief quotations embodied in critical reviews and certain other noncommercial uses permitted by copyright law. For permission requests, write to the publisher, addressed "Attention: Permissions Coordinator," at the address below.

Kimberly Moses and co-authors/Rejoice Essential Publishing

PO BOX 512

Effingham, SC 29541

www.republishing.org

Unless otherwise indicated, scripture is taken from the King James Version.'

Scripture taken from the New King James Version®. Copyright © 1982 by Thomas Nelson. Used by permission. All rights reserved.

The Holy Bible, English Standard Version® (ESV®) Copyright © 2001 by Crossway, a publishing ministry of Good News Publishers. All rights reserved.

Scripture quotations marked (NLT) are taken from the Holy Bible, New Living Translation, copyright ©1996, 2004, 2015 by Tyndale House Foundation. Used by permission of Tyndale House Publishers, Carol Stream, Illinois 60188. All rights reserved.

"Scripture quotations taken from the Amplified® Bible (AMPC), Copyright © 1954, 1958, 1962, 1964, 1965, 1987 by The Lockman Foundation Used by permission. www.lockman.org"

Scripture quotations marked JUB (or JBS) are taken from the Jubilee Bible (or Biblia del Jubileo), copyright © 2000, 2001, 2010, 2013 by Life Sentence Publishing, Inc. Used by permission of Life Sentence Publishing, Inc., Abbotsford, Wisconsin. All rights reserved.

All Things Relationships/ Kimberly Moses And Co-authors

ISBN-13: 978-1-952312-72-4

Dedication

*T*HIS BOOK WOULDN'T BE possible without the inspiration of the Holy Spirit. When I thought my life and ministry was over, He gave me another chance. I promised Him that I would help someone not to make the same mistakes. I am grateful that the Lord never gave up on me when I was at my worse.

2 Timothy 3:16-17 says, "All scripture is given by inspiration of God, and is profitable for doctrine, for reproof, for correction, for instruction in righteousness: That the man of God may be perfect, thoroughly furnished unto all good works."

— Kimberly Moses

We dedicate this book to the loving memory of our fathers, Cleveland Nelson, Jr., and Albert Clemonts, and our grandmothers, Ossie L. Jackson and Mildred M. Dryden. We also dedicate this book to our beautiful daughters, Samia Nelson,

Faith Bennett, and Kiara Clemonts. We also thank our handsome sons, Erik M. Nelson, Jr., and Be Knowledge. We dedicate this book to our beautiful mothers, Jacqueline D. Nelson and Eleanor Clemonts. Lastly, we dedicate this book to our Huddle family and The Christina Nelson Show fans.

—Erik and Christina Nelson

I delight in dedicating my two stories in this amazing book to my children, Shameike, Na'Lee, Nevaeh, Alreiana, Trinity, and my grandchildren. I am sharing my reality, triumphs, and victories. I love you all very much, with the heart of Heavenly Father God, and Christ Jesus. Children are a blessing from the Lord, and God blesses me to be a faithful steward over what my Heavenly Father has given to me. As a parent and a grandparent, if I see you making some poor choices, in love, I speak up and declare to you what is right. You do not have to compromise.

By the Spirit of God invested in me, I strongly encourage you to don't be in a relationship with a person who doesn't share nor practice your same values in Christ Jesus. Now, when the storms of life come, and they will come, what will be your compass? Whose value will you decide? When you are in Christ, you can truly answer that Father God is first in your life and at the center of your relationship. We love each other and our value in the Lord will decide.

My hope and prayer are for you all to be prayerful concerning the life partnership decisions you will make to avoid unnecessary pitfalls, hurt, deception, and lost time. I urge you to decide to make DESTINY PURPOSE-FILLED CHOICES for your life by letting the Holy Spirit lead you every step of the way. Then pass these principles of truths on to your children's children, in Christ Jesus' name. Amen.

As your mother, mentor, and witness of the Lord, my heart's desire is for you all to go down the straight and narrow path of God. Let God's will be done in your lives on earth as it is in Heaven.

With the Love of Christ Jesus,
—Love your mother Keima S. Sinclair

I want to say thank you to my Abba Father for all He has done and continues to do that made this opportunity a reality. James 1:17 says: every good gift and every perfect gift is from above, and cometh down from the Father of lights, with whom is no variableness, neither shadow of turning.

I'm dedicating my chapter on courtship to "NR." God truly graced him to stand with me through my healing process. He taught me through the wisdom that God has given him how to take life one day at a time and trust God to bring everything together in His perfect timing. I call "NR" my best friend after the Holy Spirit.

—Lavonda Gigi Love

Table of Contents

ACKNOWLEDGMENTS..xi

INTRODUCTION...1

CHAPTER 1:   Break Up
              by Irwin And Leslie Harvey....................4

CHAPTER 2:   Business
              by Kimberly Moses................................11

CHAPTER 3:   My Children Are My Future
              by Keima Shantay Sinclair....................17

CHAPTER 4:   Courtship
              by Lavonda Love......................................35

CHAPTER 5:   Family
              by Kimberly Moses................................41

CHAPTER 6:   Ministry
              by Kimberly Moses................................45

CHAPTER 7:   Reconciliation
              by Irwin "Bug" and Leslie Harvey........50

CHAPTER 8:   Restoration
              by Keima Shantay Sinclair.....................54

CHAPTER 9:   In Sickness and In Health,

	Marriage & Ministry by Erik and Christina Nelson.................87
CHAPTER 10:	Workplace by Kimberly Moses................................95

ABOUT THE AUTHORS..99

Acknowledgments

To All my co-authors, thank you. This project couldn't have taken place without your support and hard work. We all make an amazing team. I enjoyed reading each of your testimonies and I know others will enjoy it as well. Each of you brought something unique to the table as we discussed, "All Things Relationships."

—Kimberly Moses

Introduction

BY KIMBERLY MOSES

MANY RELATIONSHIPS ARE UNDERNEATH an attack: friendships, marriages, families, partners, etc. The enemy knows that there is strength in numbers.

Deuteronomy 32:30 says, "...one chase a thousand, and two put ten thousand to flight."

We aren't meant to stay on an island by ourselves. We need one another.

Hebrews 10:25 says, "Not forsaking the assembling of ourselves together, as the manner of some is; but exhorting one another: and so much the more, as ye see the day approaching."

The enemy wants us to be offended and cut off relationships with those who love and care for us. It's sad to see how many broken relationships there are in the Body of Christ. People get offended and block you just like that. They don't care that you prayed them through or encouraged them when they were at their lowest. We are all a part of the body of Christ, and we have to be our brother or sister's keeper. One strategy of the

enemy is to get you alone and isolate you, so there is no one there to pray on your behalf or encourage you.

There will be conflicts and challenges, but through Christ, we can overcome them. The enemy fights relationships of purpose. That's why your marriage or spiritual connection is going through an attack. Perhaps the enemy is trying to influence you to leave. You must rebuke the enemy and stay planted because that is where God wants you or that is who God sent to bless your life. That person has what you need for your purpose or destiny.

The divorce rate is high in the Body of Christ. Believers should be different because they have to apply God's Word as their standard for everything they do in life. God hates divorce. Some people get divorced over the most minor things. We shouldn't change spouses as we do with outfits. If we can't keep relationships with people and find ourselves running and searching, then the problem is with us. There is something broken inside that we must submit to God so He can heal us. We can prosper in our relationships when we do it God's way and build everything on the rock of Jesus Christ.

3 John 2 (ESV) says, "Beloved, I pray that all may go well with you and that you may be in good health, as it goes well with your soul."

In this book, we will cover various topics so we can have healthy relationships. It's stressful living a life of dysfunction. God wants us whole and living our best lives. We will explore

Introduction

business relationships. In business, boundaries are essential so God can get the glory. We will cover ministry relationships. It's time for the mending of spiritual connections so we can work together and advance God's Kingdom. We will delve into the impact family and marriage life have upon your assignment for God. If your household is chaotic you will not be effective in your purpose. Also, we will discuss courtship, there are so many red flags that some have chosen to ignore, and now they are miserable or hurt. Lastly, we will cover breakups and reconciliation. There is nothing too hard or impossible for God to fix.

CHAPTER 1

Break Up

BY IRWIN AND LESLIE HARVEY

THE DEFINITION OF A breakup, relationship break-up, or simply just break-up, is the termination of an intimate relationship by any means other than death. Breaking up is often termed as dumping [someone]" ("Breakup" n.d.).[1] According to Synder (2020), ending a relationship is one of the most challenging decisions made. Break-ups are caused by character differences, lack of time spent together, infidelity, communication disconnection, or lack of fulfillment within the relationship.[2]

I have ended several unsuccessful relationships as I know breakups lead us to better opportunities and healthier relationships. God says, "I know the plans that I have for you" (Jeremiah 29:11 NLT). I had been looking for love in all the wrong places. Being attracted to broken people – as they continued to

---

[1]. Break up. (n.d.) Wikipedia. Retrieved April 13, 2021, https://en.wikipedia.org/wiki/Breakup#:~:text=A%20relationship%20breakup%2C%20or%20simply%20just%20breakup%2C%20is,breakup%20is%20typically%20called%20a%20separation%20or%20divorce

[2]. Synder, Carly. (2020). 8 Ways to Feel Better After a Breakup. https://www.verywellmind.com/8-ways-to-feel-better-after-a-breakup-5089116

break me – I drew to those who were equally damaged. These actions cause recurring patterns which might challenge your faith and cause you to question yourself. But despite the sadness, you must always maintain your faith. One of God's promises is to heal the brokenhearted and bandage wounds (Psalms 147:3). I thank God for His power to heal and restore all broken hearts due to break-ups.

LESLIE'S PERSPECTIVE

I was married to the childhood sweetheart that I dated since the age of fourteen. While dating, we became sexually active instead of waiting until marriage. I had no idea about soul ties that were beginning during this time. Though married for ten years, there were multiple incidents of infidelity between both spouses. Neither one of us understood the idea or concept of marriage. After the divorce, I was broken and began leaning on my fleshly desires. As I started dating again, I was inauthentic with myself and the partners to retaliate against my ex-husband. Once we finished the sexual act, I ended the relationship. I was worried because I believed I was too old and thought nobody would want me. I told myself I would be faithful and dedicated only to my ex-husband, but he did not reciprocate those actions. I endured many broken promises from him, but I remained steadfast. I believe it hurt because friendship was not our foundation.

"It is God's will for you (us) to be holy, so stay away from all sexual sin. Then each of you will control his own body and live

in holiness and honor not in lustful passion like the pagans who do not know God's ways" (1 Thessalonians 4:3-5).

We must live to please God. When you are not in God's word or obeying God's will, you will fall. I know I was doing wrong because sin feels good. "Choosing instead suffer affliction with the people of God than to enjoy the pleasures of sin for a season" (Hebrews 11:25).

I had been engaged twice before meeting my current husband, Harvey. I prayed and asked God which man was the one. God revealed both weddings in my dreams. During the first dream, the minister asked if anyone objected and I was immediately hit with an object. But during the second dream, when I prayed and asked God about Harvey being my husband, I had such peaceful sleep.

Harvey and I dated for 18 months. He was my honey, my term of endearment, considering we were too mature to be boyfriend or girlfriend. My honey is all I could have asked for and more. My honey is hard-working, a wonderful provider, spontaneous, and thoughtful – frequently surprised me with flowers and gifts while I was providing for my own home. He is a gentleman – opening doors, which was something new to me but abundantly welcomed.

Then, following the death of his mother, he started to become distant. The lunch invitations started to decline and the phone calls were becoming infrequent, unanswered and unreturned. We began to see less and less of each other. I was confused and wondering what was happening. We went from being inseparable to not seeing or communicating at all. I saw and knew the signs we were heading towards a breakup. One day I asked him, what has happened to us? What's going on? What did I do? Is there someone else? He had no reply.

I already knew this relationship was ending as communication was non-existent. Preparing myself, I went to his home, gathered my things, returned his house key, and left. I was clueless about how we got to this point but I have been down this road too many times before. I was familiar with the shame, humiliation, pain, and hurt resulting from a breakup. My children and family loved him; yet they were each asking, what happened? I had no response because I didn't know. But now I know, I was not living and doing it God's way. I was living by the flesh and conducting the relationship my way, and it was not pleasing to Him; therefore, I suffered. The Bible clearly states, "But if they can't control themselves, they should go ahead and marry. It's better to marry than to burn with lust" (1 Corinthians 7:9). We can't blame everything on the devil. Many times we allow ourselves – our flesh – to speak to us, open and give the enemy entry to cause havoc in our lives. I know because it happened to me.

After the official breakup of the relationship, including the crying, anger, and disappointment, I began attending church. This was prompt because up to this point, I was not taking time to seek God, discover who I was in the Lord and walk in my purpose while repenting. I was committed to only dating and marrying for money, not love. I was going against everything that I said vowed to avoid. Yet, during this time, I begin seeing someone solely for what he offered financially. This man was wealthy, worked long hours and helped financially support my children and I. But I was not happy because that was not what I wanted, just settling for less than God's best.

IRWIN'S PERSPECTIVE

My mother had seven children, six sons, and one daughter, and I was the baby growing up. My oldest brother was nineteen years older than myself. My brothers and sister have been divorced more than once and had several unstable relationships during my childhood. I witness various forms of abuse, emotional, verbal, physical, and lies of deceptions.

I had a 90-day rule as I believed a person shows their true selves within 90 days of meeting them. I was not a committed person due to many breakups I encountered throughout the various relationships, letdowns, disappointment, and betrayal. I am not perfect; I also had my ways of helping the relationship not to flourish or go to the next level.

During my first marriage, my first wife and I separated when my firstborn was six months old. The breakup ended in divorce because of an argument that led to physical and verbal violence. I was in the army during the time of the allegations, and I was arrested and jailed. My superior officer was called, and I was given two choices 1) to send her home or 2) face charges – the military frowns upon any abuse of spouses.

Break Up

I sent my ex-wife home and then the divorce was filed. I was in my early twenties. There was no connection. Therefore, I felt nothing – no emotion – just a clean break up which allowed me to move on with my life.

My second marriage didn't last long either; there were many infidelities, verbal, physical, and emotional abuse. We were granted favor because when the police were called, the officer that arrived was a prior schoolmate, so no arrests were made. After two years of marriage, we determined divorce was best. Unsure as to why my marriages didn't last, I was a traditional member of the church and unfamiliar with God's word. Once again, I felt nothing – no emotion – just a clean break up which allowed me to move on with my life.

All of my relationships were temporary, short- term due to the women I was attracted to who wanted to use me for my money to purchase cars, assist with helping their family, paying for child care, or legal matters. You name it, they asked and I gave. Their motives were not to be a long-term commitment, only until the giving stop or I got tired and moved on to the next. I was deceived numerous times. Therefore, when the relationship ended, I felt no remorse.

Why did I give? I gave because I am a giver to those in need. My parents were givers. This was inherited. I believed the lies they told me.

I was in my thirties. I was casually dating and cycling through various relationships absolved from commitment. During this time, I was in the military, so I would frequently travel and move between states and reside in various countries. After my overseas return, I was introduced to Leslie by a family member who spoke highly of her. We met at a birthday celebration. Leslie had no clue her co-worker was setting her up.

We met for the first time; there was no connection. Then we were reintroduced and began dating after eighteen months. While dating, although we never talked about marriage, we were committed to the relationship, but I simply was not ready. Therefore, I decided to end the relationship and headed back to the streets and partying, chasing women and drinking. This was familiar to me; this was a world that I enjoyed and did not plan on leaving anytime soon.

I was in church all the time, not learning, not studying, only because it was all I knew. I was a traditional member, just going through the motions.

Throughout my life, whenever I date the person who showed a side of being untrue and not willing to commit, I left to prevent myself from being hurt. Constantly rejoicing in hope [because of our confidence in Christ], steadfast and patient in distress, devoted to prayer [continually seeking wisdom, guidance, and strength](Romans 12:12 Amplified Bible).

In conclusion, can you heal from a break-up? The answer is yes, you can!

CHAPTER 2

Business

BY KIMBERLY MOSES

I NEVER THOUGHT THAT GOD would allow me to have businesses. When I said yes to the calling on my life in 2014, I was still working as a Registered Respiratory Therapist. I was traveling to different hospitals and had aspirations of becoming a Medical doctor in the future. However, as I grew closer to the Lord, doors closed for me to pursue a path in medicine. God was directing me to do full-time ministry and I had to go through several trials. My work hours at the hospital were cut and I could barely pay my bills. Every time I got on social media or spoke to someone, they would give me a prophecy that God was going to call me to do full-time ministry.

For about two years, I was doing ministry on the prayer line and social media; but in 2016, I got terminated from my job because they found out that I was on probation. It was devastating, but at that moment, God spoke to me and said that I was now in the office of a prophet and not to be afraid. Amazingly, money came in supernaturally and I was able to pay bills. Yet, there was still a struggle there and sometimes my money was funny.

I ran into a company of false prophets who were money-hungry. They pimped God's people and everything was about raising money, not about glorifying Jesus. My husband, Tron, who I was in courtship with at the time, warned me about these prophets. Tron didn't want me to be influenced by them or have my image tainted. I took heed and disconnected.

I began to seek God for a way not to struggle. I was tired of prophesying to people when I was broke. I was tired of getting food from the food bank. Worse off, I wanted to move out of the bad environment I lived in. I just wanted my children and I to be financially stable. God promised me that He was going to take care of me. Soon after, a friend of mine came up to me in church and gave me a prophecy about me having a business doing something that I am already anointed to do and the financial struggle was over.

I went back home after service and prayed about the prophecy. Suddenly, God gave me the idea to start a publishing company. In 2017, Rejoice Essential Publishing was a legitimate entity. This company was an expansion of Rejoice Essential Magazine, which was birthed in 2015. I had already written around 12 books and was praying for about twenty-five thousand dollars to get them published. Then God spoke to me one day and said, "Publish them yourself." So I started my publishing journey. I researched and studied the field. I made sure everything was done in excellence. As I began releasing my books, people started noticing and came to me for services. Along the way, I had a few difficult clients and some who tried to take

Business

over the business or expected me to give them free work. God always strengthens me for this journey so I could be a good steward over it.

In March 2020, COVID-19 was starting to claim many lives in North America. The country was in fear and shutdowns were enforced. God spoke to me one day and told me to start a beauty business. Rejoicing Beauty was created and God began to blow on it. Every time I did a video or posted a photo, the sales would come in. I didn't understand why God wanted me, as a minister, to enter into that realm. Now I know that I am called to be a light in a dark place. There is a lot of perversion in the beauty industry. I see men wearing bundles, wigs, lashes, shapers, etc. Most of the known brands are strong advocates of the LGBTQ+ movement. God needs Kingdom business in the world to represent Jesus.

WISDOM

1. Don't compromise

You can be saved and love Jesus but be called to business. Apostle Paul was a tentmaker (Acts 18:1-4). He didn't have to worry about money or having impure motives. His focus was Jesus and he didn't look at people as a dollar sign. One of the benefits of having my own business is that I can do ministry without motives. Whether people donate to my ministry or not, I'm blessed. God will take care of me and allow me to be blessed in other ways. You never want to compromise or grieve the Holy Spirit. Stay true to the message or brand that God has

given you. We can't follow the crowd or do what's popular to get cash. I had to turn away books that people wanted me to publish that were full of sex, curse words, and sorcery. I can't have certain shirts on my beauty site because I represent Jesus. When you glorify God in your business, He will bless it.

2. You are worth your rate

I have a set rate and it barely changes. Some people have come to me trying to cut deals like a hustler. You must know that your God-given business is not to be hustled. It is another income source to generate wealth in your life so you can leave a legacy for your family. Some people don't want to pay you because it's you or they don't value what you have to offer. They don't mind paying someone else. If they don't want to pay your prices, God will send people who will invest in your services. If you continue to give away free services all the time, then some people won't buy from you or take you seriously. They will spend their money elsewhere.

One of my mentees was pouring out for hours on the phone with a few women. She was helping them get their businesses started and doing some consulting work. The only problem was that she was doing it for free and she was broke. She couldn't afford food, was behind on her bills, and couldn't provide for her children. I told her to stop giving away her services for free because she was worth her rate. She listened to me and money started flowing. Now her calendar is booked for most of the year.

3. Be a good steward over it

Surprisingly, I had to guard my business against other Christians who had the wrong spirits. They would've taken over if I was passive and didn't stand up. One person came to me and was critical of everything I did. My businesses are a part of my ministry, but this individual was rude, overbearing, and offended. They felt like they knew everything and didn't take heed of my expertise. When there was a grammatical error in the manuscript, if I corrected it, they got offended and talked bad about me to some peers trying to destroy my character. It got to the point where I had to get a mediator involved or a trusted individual to work with this person because everything that I did was wrong in their sight. Since they were difficult to work with, I had to restrict their access to me. I knew that it was the enemy trying to speak evil of my well-doing. God didn't allow what the enemy was trying to do through this person to work. He sent me an influx of clientele who spoke highly of my services.

4. Pray over your business

I learned to always pray over my businesses for the right clientele because the Lord's blessings make you rich and add no sorrow (Proverbs 10:22). All money isn't good money. If it's going to stress me or give me a headache, I don't want it. I rather keep the peace that Jesus gave me to be effective in what I'm called to do. I always pray for God to protect my businesses from demonic attacks and to prosper me. During the pandemic, God made sure that we didn't struggle and sent clientele regularly. We even made a profit while other businesses were filing bankrupt. I yield my businesses unto God and He always warns me when He doesn't want me to connect with a person. Once I didn't listen to a dream God gave me. The dream was about a crooked individual trying to connect and ended up hurt in the end. I repented for my disobedience. Listen to God because the enemy comes to kill, steal, and destroy.

CHAPTER 3

My Children Are My Future

BY KEIMA SHANTAY SINCLAIR

MY STORY EXPOUNDS ON the blessings and challenges of having my children, my growth as a mother, and the person who matured in who God called me to be today. Children are a gift from God. The Heavenly Father does not want us to abstain from marriage, but be fruitful, multiply, and populate the earth. I remember growing up. I acted out and my mother would put me on punishment. That is the just consequence I faced. If my mom had seemed to run out of patience with me, she took me to my grandparents' house. My grandmother was one of the sweetest and unconditional loving persons I know. She had so much care and understanding and all of the patience in the world with me. My grandmother would pray for us, anointing us with olive oil and always encouraging our entire family by declaring, "Keep looking up," while looking and pointing up to Heaven. She is right to point us back to God our Father, who is our everything. Psalm 121:1-2 says, "I will lift up my eyes unto the hills from where comes our help, our help comes from the LORD which made Heaven and earth." Amen.

I often wondered why my children, especially my oldest and two younger ones, misbehaved in such a corrupt manner. As they became teenagers, they would either purposely delay following the instructions I gave them to do or be very disrespectful by raising their voices, talking back, slamming doors, stomping their feet, and even cursing. I called it as I saw it – plain EVIL! I let them know that I love them very much and the Heavenly Father loves us most. I show them grace and mercy as God has shown me grace and mercy. I will never tell them anything wrong and instruct them not to disobey God's commands or break the law. I tell them to do the right things to be successful and have great achievements in their lives to the glory of God our Father.

SELF-EXAMINATION

I wish I had made better choices regarding my relationships and be particular about who I had let be around my first son, surrounding him with good influence and character. I did not heed to wise counsel and advice concerning my decision to get married and to whom. Equally important, I had to confess my faults and forgive myself and others who have hurt me in my life so that I can be forgiven. Otherwise, self-pity and deep regret have led to thoughts and desires of not wanting to live a life like this any longer were setting in my mind and breeding other negative thoughts. The devil is a liar! There is no truth in him.

Growing up, I never dreamed of having a big family because I had dreams of traveling the world, doing great exploits for the Kingdom of God and being a business owner. It was my ex-husband's desire to have a lot of children and for me to stay home and raise them. I came in agreement to please him and fulfill his heart's desires. Having my children with God on my side has been miraculous in so many ways as I continue to trust in Him. By the way, being a housewife with children and a 3-month-old, God still made a way for me and opened the door to allow me to travel the world. I did not have any money of my own! God is a way maker. He is the door! That is the power of God! No one can stop what God has in store for you. His favor is matchless.

As a divorcee, I have made it a priority and my business to find ways to relate to their father and make peace with him and build a friendship for the sake of our children. When their father gets out of line by saying or doing things that can be very disturbing and corrupt, I don't always respond well. I have gotten in the flesh (carnal mind) several times, out of my character. But I made up my mind and I know who I am and who I belong to. I live for God and my life I have given to Him to use me purposefully for His glory. Therefore, my life is not my own because I belong to Him. With that, I will go to my children's father to make it right with him, asking for forgiveness as well as forgiving him. Then the next thing I know, his temper has calmed and we are laughing and making plans with our children together. This is the example our children need and should expect from us as parents if we make a mistake or consciously make the wrong decision, purposely saying bad things to each other. I have matured much, yielding my fleshly ways to

God for Him to help me through family matters and be an overcomer. He comes to my rescue when I lean on Him because He is my helper, deliverer, shield, buckler, and protector. I learned not to be foolish and argue with my children's dad, especially in front of our children.

One of my ex-sister-in-laws expressed to my cousin what she is going through with her son is because of their side of the family. I shared some of the heartache and disappointments that I experienced as well. I thought, "Finally, an honest confession," which was very helpful and brought healing. As a result, we gained an understanding of this generational pattern and how to still provide our unconditional love as parents. We will support them in this special area of need and deal patiently with them for their deliverance.

While taking our discipline to our children to another level according to Biblical principles and praying our spiritual warfare prayers effectively, we took the time to understand what our children are going through and recognize the spiritual attacks on their lives. I was able to fight the good fight of faith better and take what I learned by hearing Bible teachings and revelation of the Word of God from the pastor, church and fellowship with other believers. I received and used that anointed power to help fuel me throughout the week for my children and me. Without doing so, I realized that it could get quite chaotic in our home.

According to God's Word, I have prayed, fasted, and interceded for my children and God did wonders. I have also joined prayer groups and submitted prayer requests on their behalf. If I am not doing what I am supposed to do but I know that waiting on God is helping. Even if I do not see instant results, I know that things are not bad as they could be without Him. When I believe His Word and believe for His hand to deal with my family circumstances, I am focused. When I get off track, I notice the difference and I do not want to displease the Heavenly Father or grieve His Holy Spirit. I want to be sensitive to the Spirit of God, not leaving the door open for the enemy to come in and wreak havoc on our minds or try to have my children turn against me as if I was their enemy. There is power in praying. If I do not have a prayer life, there is no authentic, lasting power and I won't have adequate strength to fight the enemy. God's Word and doing what He says has blessed my children and me over the years; no matter what trial or tribulation we have faced, we can do all things in Christ that strengthens us. Jesus Christ said when two or more gathered in His name, He is in the midst (among) of us and if two or three are touching and agreeing on asking anything in prayer, He said it shall be done for us of His Father who is in Heaven. God remains faithful in our family situations and He sees us through to the breakthrough we need. He has never failed us yet.

Raising up our children in the fear, reverence, and admonition of God eventually reaps a good and orderly harvest of righteous living for them and peace for us parents! They will know God for themselves and have the wisdom they need from day to day in their upbringing.

"Every word of God is pure: he is a shield unto them that put their trust in him." – Proverbs 30:5

"My son, attend to my words; incline thine ear unto my sayings. Let them not depart from thine eyes; keep them in the midst of thine heart. For they are life unto those that find them, and health to all their flesh. Keep thy heart with all diligence; for out of it are the issues of life." – Proverbs 4:20-23

HOLDING ON STRONG AND FIGHTING THE GOOD FIGHT

Every time a terrible situation occurs at school regarding my children, I let their father know what is going on and let them converse with him. He lets them know to do better and not do it again. He also asks why they did what they have done and that is good. He may not always say the right things when talking with them. But I am reminded that he is not on his knees yet in prayer and communing with the Heavenly Father to give his children the sound wisdom and godly instruction they need.

Whether my children are being bullied, retaliating against others, or getting into a heated confrontation, I immediately agree for them to go into mediation to work things out between their peers to learn how to respect one another and treat each other how they want to be treated. If that doesn't seem to help much, I request counseling if their School Counselor doesn't write up a referral for counseling. If something more is needed, I will write letters following the chain of command. That way, my intentions and expressions of my concerns regarding my children's safety, monitoring and protection are precise and to the point.

When a teacher is having a bad day, we sometimes let it go, forgive them and pray about it because they are human just like we are. On the other hand, if a teacher, lunch monitor, or school official is out of line consistently and I can see that they are letting the spirit of the devil use them, I will pray about it and I'll firmly confront them and defend my children. I am their mother and I am to protect my children with all that's within me. When my children are right, they are right and they get praised and rewarded accordingly. When they are wrong, they are wrong and should be given a warning and be reprimanded, given consequences for their actions and learn to be responsible for their actions. Nevertheless, I command them in love, yet courageously to do right by us and treat us in the same manner and likeness they want to be treated and for the school system to find ways to relate to my children and for a peaceful resolution.

Unfortunately, a few certain individuals in my children's public school have decided in their heart's not to deal with my complaints or any correction I bring to them. I have provided sound Biblical principles or legal fight of defense representing and advocating on my children's behalf and bringing other people with a good and strong reputation in the community involved to observe the unfairness and corruption going on and stand with me in this fight. With that, I was still reported falsely to the 'Children and Families Division of Youth and Family

Services,' which the process can be a nightmare and very hard on some parent(s), especially if they bombarded by the system unfairly and are innocent, have been accused, and do not know what to do without legal counsel or the Lord's intervention. But as for me, I was ready to fight a good fight of faith and stand for my rights and back my children so we can see the salvation of the Lord! Although I was fired up and eager to prove my case, I humbly asked God what I should do? I sensed in my spirit that I could pray and use my authority over the real enemy (Satan) in secret with God and He will reward me openly. I asked others who are intercessory spiritual prayer warriors to pray for me. I was also blessed to have an idea to speak their language and communicate in the way they know I can relate to them and vice versa. The next step I took was I downloaded and studied the manual 18A:12-24.1 Code of Ethics for School Board Members on the State's Board of Education and other Policies from the Department of Education's website and HIB (Harassment, Intimidation and Bullying). Additional bullying resources were being given to me when I reached out to an independent local Parent Advocate Agency. I got educated and read how School officials took an oath to follow the Code of Ethics as educators. Well, a few of my children's teachers, etc. had broken several of them. Yet, they weren't being reprimanded. Instead, they covered for one another or swept certain things under the rug, not caring about the concerns of a parent or their student.

I reviewed the information and procedures and saw how they conducted their reporting and review of a child. They labeled each child based on their emotion or behavior, the type of study interventions and evaluations, and the State's child psychology they offered. When I spoke about God to them and His love, mercy, goodness, wisdom, and how I raise my children to know His ways and to treat others as they want to be treated, they called me radically religious. They labeled and reported me as having mental health issues, erratic behavior, and substance abuse in their observation. I was shocked and hurt they could do such a thing. And so, I fought the system's policy that sets a date to have this testing done, and I was more than willing to cooperate, but sooner than later. Glory to God, I have found favor to immediately test since I have been accused of such things. My mother, father, uncle, and other family members stood by my side to help me in this fight. I am so forever grateful for them, their prayers, and for coming with me to the school and board meetings. But for the most part, I had to fight alone a lot of times. I decided not to drag them into my fight every time and trust God.

I used the wisdom God gave me, such as to record every meeting with their acknowledgment. God let me know that I have my rights and I can turn down certain recommendations they had in mind for my child that may end up keeping them bound in the system under the wrong impression, simply because they could not relate to my child. And so, when I was evaluated and took the tests, I received nothing but good news. I do not promote violence and I do not condone my child to retaliate and be disrespectful to anyone. Children are children and they will make mistakes as they are growing and developing into the person God made them to be. My God gave me peace. He turned things around and the outcome was in my favor so much that when the CFDYFS investigated and saw the evidence and that I was truthful, my case was closed, and unfounded, twice! Glory to God! Rumors began and there was a fear I was going to sue the school for physical damages and defamation of character, slander, etc. My children started receiving gifts and money from the teachers and security guards. They were being treated with great respect and dignity. At one point in time, I did seek legal counsel to know my legal rights etc., but I could not afford an attorney, so I continued to put my trust in Father God in Jesus' mighty name to give me a miracle from these unjust, malicious, and messy cases brought up against me. I praise His Holy name! When I seemed to have gotten tired, God gave me strength. When I did not want to keep on fighting, God gave me hope. I was told several times that I do not look like what I have been through! Praise God Almighty, who is my keeper and who never left my side! God promises His children that when we pass through the waters, He will be with us; and through the rivers, they shall not overflow or overtake us: when we walk through the fire, we shall not be burned; neither shall the flame kindle upon us.

I continue to pray for other parents and families who may be struggling in this area and they may be guilty and ought to get the help they need. God, our maker, is our provider and will provide our needs through the powerful name Christ Jesus! Seek after God with all your heart and strength and He will never lead you wrong, but He is willing to teach us and comfort us and love on us like no one ever has. He is a good God and He will see us through! There is nothing too that's hard for God to do for us, His beloved children. And as long as we ask God to help us and put it in our hearts to genuinely forgive those who wronged us, He will forgive us of our sins.

Blessed is the man that trusteth in the LORD, and whose hope the LORD is. For he shall be as a tree planted by the waters, and that spreadeth out her roots by the river, and shall not see when heat cometh, but her leaf shall be green; and shall not be careful in the year of drought, neither shall cease from yielding fruit.– Jeremiah 17:7-8

Nay, in all these things we are more than conquerors through him that loved us.– Romans 8:37

HEAVENLY STRATEGIES

And all thy children shall be taught of the Lord; and great shall be the peace of thy children. – Isaiah 54:13

Surprisingly, a late Pastor blessed me with my first Children's Bible two decades ago, which I have taught my children from. I still have the same Children's Bible today, although it's not in top condition. It's readable. It has become a way of life for me and a joy to read the Bible to them where they can understand at their tender age and when they got a little older. I instruct them to read the Children's Bible (God's Living Word) for themselves on their own. I love it when they read the Bible out loud and we all hear the Word of God and our home is filled with the peace of God. It is such a blessing and I have seen the fruit of being consistent and meditating upon His truth for our lives.

The Children's Bible given to me by the late Pastor is special and unique. It contains not only Bible stories with Scripture but easy to understand and comprehend. It has prayer and memory verses to help children confess God's Word and help them remember it. For me, it was an effective teaching tool in addition to them going to Children's Sunday school. The Pastor was a mother and led her children in the things of God by this single gift I received from her of a Children's Bible. She encouraged and helped me teach my children independently God's ways to develop their own relationship with Him to get to know who He is in their lives. By doing so, I have learned more about God myself.

Starting with my oldest child, I would have him read God's promises. I wanted him to know how much he is loved by God and the things God desires to do to bless us. I guide my children to read and pray the Bible passages and stories not only every day, but when they are in error, not obeying authority, or being disrespectful to me. I give God the Glory for helping me to strategize and incorporating His Holy Word into their lives even if they have done wrong. This method has helped calm their spirits, redirect their thinking, and bring correction to them for the health, wellbeing, and strength of their mind, body, and soul. And so, for part of their punishment, this is what I have instructed them to do. God is faithful because it works! God has also put strangers, angels, wise people, women and men of God in our lives to speak life into our dark situations. Where there seems to be little hope left, God is always on time to pull us right up out of that messy situation or give us the strength to endure to the end of that thing.

About five years ago, all hell seemed to break loose. None of the children were doing right at home and I gave my mom a call about these matters. She responded, letting me know I needed to play Gospel music continually and praised God because that spirit in them is of the enemy and the devil cannot stay. He has to flee. And so, the first time I did this, my children calmed down. Praise God! One of my daughters even started singing along with the Gospel music. The devil was out of our dwelling! Thank you, Jesus!

SETTING THE STANDARDS

I encouraged my children years ago to rewrite and change the lyrics to songs they like and make them righteous to be a blessing for them and others who hear them sing and rap. Today they are singing and making Godly music of their own. God is good! He is great and greatly to be praised. As I am searching for different Christian melodies to listen to for praise and worship, I've discovered young musicians that sing and rap for children. My children can groove to and get godly influence. They enjoy it, asking me to play it again or asking the name of the song. God created music and it belongs to Him. There are various styles and creativity in music and I inform my children it is what we offer up to God and honor and glorify Him that makes the difference.

I look for Christian movies and true stories on the media apps I can stream on my TV or on my devices while traveling with my children. I discovered that there are so many edifying and encouraging movies for my children and adults alike. I share this information with many others to bless them and their loved ones, church family, and friends. Having access to these affordable spiritual tools is a way for my outreach ministry that began with teaching and sharing with my children, niece, nephews, children's friends, and children in my communities in New York and New Jersey. I thank the Lord for enabling me to equip my children and other children with God's truth through media and music, etc. I am blessed to be a parent and good steward over them. They know God and they can turn to their Heavenly Father for any situation or circumstance. They know that God will help them achieve anything they believe for Him to do.

Planting these seeds of righteousness and holiness must yield a blessing of harvest with every one of my children in Jesus' name.

"Let your light so shine before men, that they may see your good works, and glorify your Father which is in heaven." – Matthew 5:16

"But as He (The Father in heaven) which hath called you is holy, so be ye holy in all manner of conversation; Because it is written, Be ye holy; for I am holy." – 1 Peter 1:15-16

"Every good and perfect gift comes from the Father above; whom have no variableness nor shadow of turning."– James 1:17

My relationship with my children grew stronger and when conflict arises, things are peacefully resolved more quickly than it has in the past. Glory be to God for that! I have a part that I have to fulfill, pursuing God and taking what we are going through in prayer directly to Him in Christ Jesus. I can go straight to the throne room because God is alive. He is not Dead! The more hungry and thirsty I get for the things of God and to live right in His sight, I read the Bible and search for historical stories where God has moved powerfully on behalf of His people who obeyed Him and trusted in Him with confidence. I search the Scriptures for wisdom, and He speaks to me, and it is right on time! God does all of the rest supernaturally. He moves by His Spirit to work things out and I cannot always see what or how He does what He is doing. This is not my job. It is only to depend on His goodness and faithfulness to favorably work out my family matters and those who demonically come against us.

Stress is hard on the body system and the immune system can weaken, causing illness or disease, especially if there is a family history of health issues. I have been there and experienced sickness when my children have aggravated me to the point that my blood pressure was very high and I could not get out of bed, and I had to go to the hospital. I called on the saving grace and mercy of the Lord Jesus to first forgive me of any sins I have committed, seen and unseen, of omissions and commissions against Him. I asked that He heal me in my body and it

seemed like my dizziness and head and vision pain were getting worse. Then after a while, the Lord gave me a vision with me leaving the hospital without needing any serious care or treatment. I believed it was possible with all of my heart and in about 40 minutes, I felt led to get up by faith, and as I started to move, I felt much better. I could walk without my head pounding, causing me not to stand up for long periods at a time.

So, if I take problems on myself, I am trying to figure out the root of the problem and find a solution. It sometimes risks me getting out of character and lashing out at my children. But, if I get in the Spirit and stay in the Spirit, I am letting God take the wheel. I get in the Spirit by putting on the mind of Christ and operate in the fruits of the Spirit, which is love, peace, joy, etc. Another way I get in the Spirit is by allowing God's power to flow through me and allowing His Spirit to lead me and give me wisdom. He has His perfect way in my circumstances. He is a miracle worker! Every time God seems to arrest my children's spirits and those bring drama to our family. We have the victory through Jesus Christ and Him alone!

During my research on children's thinking, mood swings, and behaviors, a study was done on increased weapon and street violence activity. In almost every case, each gang member had a similar related story due to fatherlessness:

- Runaways
- School dropouts
- Children on drugs
- Young adults in prison

- Teen pregnancies

I had to take time with my children one by one to find out what motivates them. So, I could put a plan in place and have counsel with a few trusted and mature believers in Christ concerning my children. I have found ways and strategies to help them and simultaneously, it improves their behavior. Plus, I have incorporated a healthier eating style for them with natural foods and teas to help with chemical imbalance and mood-enhancing. God gave us fruits and herbs for food and the leaves of the trees heal nations. However, seek what you should do concerning your health in prayer and consult with your medical doctor and natural doctor. I have a disclaimer that I am not advising anyone reading my testimony to try or take any supplementation of any kind. Please do your own research and seek medical attention immediately, if needed.

Father God is no respecter of persons. In the same manner, He is helping me to raise my children. He can do the same for any parent who is willing to surrender and yield their family problems that seem too difficult to bear to Him. God will not put more on you than you can bare. I heard this a thousand times, "What doesn't kill you, makes you stronger." Or you will be just a living, walking, a miserable and hopeless person every day of your life. But it doesn't have to be this way. God can do exceedingly abundantly all we can ask or think according to the power that is in us. All we have to do is receive God's love inside of your heart. Confess to Him your situation, leave it there with the Lord and trust Him to handle it all. Go to a Bible-believing sanctuary and be encouraged and filled with the Spirit of God as you receive Him in your heart. Jesus invites us to come to Him, all of us who labored and are heavy ladened, and He will give us rest. His desire for us is to take His yoke upon us and learn of Him. For He is meek and lowly. Lowly means having low esteem of one's own worth; humble; meek; free from pride of heart. We shall find rest unto our souls. When we come to Jesus Christ with our burdens and cares, His yoke is easy and His burden is light, and we rest better in Him.

It is my motherly duty to set the standards that they need to aim for in life. My prayers are that I decree and declare this cycle of abandonment and time lost in a father and his children's relationship will be no more. Whatever patterns we set for our children would likely be set for our children and the generations after that. Fathers have the responsibility also to mold and shape their children. A father is needed to be present and visual to teach a child to be responsible and productive young men and women in society. Through experience, when a father is not present, God will make a way to stand in the gap and bring comfort and healing. Trust and believe God, for He is worthy.

"I am the LORD who heals you." – Exodus 15:26 ~

CHAPTER 4

Courtship

BY LAVONDA LOVE

AT MY AGE, I didn't have a clue what I was doing. Therefore, the fear of doing the wrong thing almost paralyzed me. I made up my mind six years ago that I was doing things the way God wanted me to because my way just was not getting me where I needed or wanted to be. So, I focused on myself and making things right for my children. Stay with me. I'm going to take you somewhere.

According to definitions from Oxford Languages, courting is a verb and it means to be involved romantically, typically with the intention of marrying. Also, it means to pay special attention to someone in an attempt to win their support or favor. I'm a sixty's baby and the church really didn't teach about courting or anything else for that matter other than "DON'T DO IT." "It" was sex and if you did it, you would get pregnant. After finding myself single again as a result of being divorced two times, I was done. I did not want anyone bothering me and I was not going to bother anyone. I was just tired and wanted something different.

After moving to Jacksonville, Florida, in April 2017, the first prophetic word I received was: "God said He is sending you a husband." I cried at the altar not because I was happy, but because I was upset. I felt like God was trying to get rid of me and I wanted it to just stay me and Him. We are so good together. I rejected that prophecy from my heart boldly. I said: "I DON'T WANT NO HUSBAND -PERIODT!!!!!" I did that two times and it didn't work, so it's insane to keep doing something over and over and it's not working. I told God I was ready for something new, something I had never done before. I knew I could not handle heartbreak again so I had to protect myself even if that meant I had to stay by myself. I was so afraid.

God is such a loving Father indeed that He allowed me to talk cash trash for a few months, but He called me to the floor and told me: "you offended me." I was so hurt that I offended the one that I loved so much. I never wanted to hurt Him because without Him, I had nobody. I hurriedly asked Him how I offended Him? He said, "You rejected my gift to you." I said, "How?" He said when I told you I was sending you your husband, you rejected what I said. He then told me that I could not hide behind my love for Him out of fear of being hurt again. He said: I told you that I was sending you a husband. Do you think I will send you a husband that would hurt you or break your heart? He said, "I am doing this and not you." I repented and I told Him that I would accept whoever He sent. I had forgotten that the last part of the prophecy said that I would reject him at first, but God would show me that He sent him. Lol! I have learned a lot about myself. One very important thing is that I have running in my feet. My God! I'm a runner.

After that encounter, I went on about my way, striving to do what I was supposed to be doing for God to be glorified in me. My main assignment was nursing school. I did not know that completing nursing school was a part of His master plan to cause my husband and I to meet. God does everything with purpose. There is no wasted time or opportunities. It gives Him great pleasure to give us good gifts. He told me that he would be everything I ever wanted in a man because my ways pleased Him. I am humbled for Him to tell me my ways please Him because Hebrew 11:6 tells us without faith, it is impossible to please Him. Pleasing God is my daily desire.

Through my courting journey, I have learned some very valuable nuggets that I will share with you.

WISDOM

1. We need wisdom to date.

Proverbs 4:7 teaches that wisdom will tell you that it's not wise to plaster everything on social media. Things need time to grow and mature because everybody in your friend's list is not happy for you.

2. Patience will get you to your final destiny.

James 1: 4 says, "But let patience have her perfect work, that ye may be perfect and entire, wanting nothing." When God is working, we need patience to not rush things and cause a disas-

ter. Just because you are getting along with a person does not mean you should run to that altar or courthouse. Everything needs time.

3. Everything has a set time.

Galatians 4:4 says, "But when the fullness of time had come, God sent forth His Son." You see, even Jesus had a set time to come. He could not come too early or too late because that could have hindered the plan of the Father. We also must remember that God is in control and not us. He tells us what to do and we do not tell Him. He truly knows best. The Holy Spirit gave me this analogy about the importance of things working according to the Father's plan. The instructions for Pillsbury buttermilk biscuits say to cook them at the temperature of 375 for 40 minutes. Well because we want them now, we cook them at 400 for 20 minutes. They look brown on the outside, but the middle is not fully cooked. We eat them and end up with a severe belly ache and nausea. Those biscuits are no good for anyone. Resting in God's timing is the only way to have VICTORY.

4. Pride can destroy and cause you to miss your blessing.

James 4:6 says, "But He giveth more grace. Wherefore He saith, God resisteth the proud, but giveth more grace to the humble." I almost missed Him because I had pride. The Holy Spirit checked me A.K.A. jacked me up by the collar. He said, "You are full of yourself. You think the only reason a man can want you is because you are a RN? You haven't always been one." I repented and humbled myself. A lot of women and men look down on the one God sends because they may not be on their level in so many areas. But God will always send us who we need to help us grow. Sometimes we set goals and once we have reached them, we feel so accomplished that God cannot do anything with us. A person on a different level gives us more space to grow. Never judge a book by its cover. You will be surprised what you find when you open it.

5. Purging and Washing.

Psalms 51:7 says, "Purge me with hyssop, and I shall be clean: wash me, and I shall be whiter than snow." I learned that the most important part of courting is to get to really see yourself. I had things that I thought were over, but the Holy Spirit has used and continued to use my friend to wash me in the Word as He purges me. He has rebuked, chastised, and loved me through prayer into healing. He sees me and my flaws and refuses to leave. I see areas that he needs to be strengthened in too, therefore, I pray for him; we pray for each other. There is nothing wrong with spending time talking, but please do not neglect praying for each other and the secret place. A lot of things can be fixed before marriage if we allow the Holy Spirit to lead us.

6. Seeking the kingdom.

Matthew 6:33 says, "But seek first the kingdom of God, and his righteousness; and all these things shall be added unto you." You will not fail if you are both fulfilling this word. God will give you His plan for your marriage and grace you to stand the test of times. Take your time and find out what His Kingdom purpose is and when the enemy comes, you will be prepared.

7. Take time to know the person.

Genesis 4:1 says, "And Adam knew Eve his wife, and she conceived." Let us go deeper on the knowing. While praying, ask God to let your spirits meet. If you only know each other after the flesh, you will not last. When you know each other by the spirit, you will know how to strategically pray the will of God over his or her life. You can also pray and prophesy them into their Kingdom purpose. There will be plenty of time for the fleshly encounter. First things first. When we put God at the head, we will never go wrong. I decree and declare that His Kingdom come and His will be done in your life as you read my story in Jesus' name. Shalom!

CHAPTER 5

Family

BY KIMBERLY MOSES

Family is the most important relationship that we will ever have. When no one has your back, they will be there. It will do us no good if we are trying to save the world, but our families hate ministry or want nothing to do with church because of our actions. When I got arrested, my sister and her husband drove thirteen hours to bail me out of jail. They came to pick up my SUV from my ex-husband, who hated me at the time and they parked it right in front of the jailhouse so I could have a ride home after I was processed out. When my ex-husband kicked me out on the streets, my parents drove twenty-five hours to help me find an apartment. My family has always gone above and beyond to be there for me.

When I got remarried, I had a hard time balancing my time, especially with my children. I was always preaching and my children needed me. Once my daughter had a concert, I dropped her off but didn't come inside because I had to do ministry. My daughter was really upset with me because I missed her big moment. I had put ministry before her and I had to repent. That was the last time that I did that. I prayed for help and the Lord sent me a wonderful group of women to help me in ministry so I didn't have to do everything myself. Moses had to delegate and God took his spirit and divided it upon the seventy elders. If Moses didn't have assistance, he would've continued to minister from sunup to sundown (Numbers 11:16-30). There must be a balance.

One day I preached on my Wedding Anniversary. I was so anxious for an opportunity to preach the gospel, so when a door opened, I jumped on it. I wasn't thinking about how it made him feel. He agreed for me to minister because he never wants to get between God and me. However, I knew it made him feel some kind of way. The sad part is that I no longer talk to the person who invited me to minister. God had to show me that my husband comes first. It will do me no good if I'm giving out so much and praying others to break through while my personal life falls apart.

Even though my family supports me, there is a line that I have to be careful to cross. Sometimes, I have offended them when I told my full testimony. It is my truth and they don't want others to know what we really went through. I was surprised when I discovered they listen to me minister. That shows that my family truly supports what I do. Many people have experienced a fall out in their family because of the revealing of the family business. However, God can help, restore, and mend broken relationships.

When I get disappointed and hurt, my husband is there to encourage me. He prays for me when I am going through a spiritual attack. He is always there as I go forth in my calling.

God says that two are better than one. We have a good reward for our labor. Everyone needs someone in their amen corner. Rejection is common among ministers, especially prophets. So God gave me a spouse who gives me the attention and support that I need. In return, I must give my spouse the same, so I learned to date him. We have to spend time together often. We find something that we like to do and build memories. We invest in our marriage. We pray, fast, travel, eat, and flirt. I will be more effective when my personal life is peaceful and orderly, so I can help others achieve the same.

I have to spend time with my children. They need attention so I can ensure they aren't hanging with the wrong crowd or doing something on social media that they have no business doing. They are growing up and have feelings. They need the wisdom that God has placed on my life to help them make the best choices in life. I don't want my kids to be churched out or hate it because I'm always doing ministry. Instead, I let them see how fun serving God is by allowing them to experience the travel, testimonies, and the presence of God. I want them to develop a relationship with God on their own.

WISDOM

1. Family first

If you don't put your family first, they won't be around when you need them the most. You don't want to die alone because you push everyone away or didn't make your loved ones a priority. You can't save the world when your house is a mess. Your family needs you and family should be your first ministry. I delegate my prayer assignments, so I can be a wife who keeps the house clean and puts hot meals on the table. I have administrative assistants and editors for my businesses, so I can enjoy time with my children. I don't want my children to resent me because I gave their time away to others. Motherhood is one of my greatest joys. There are too many divorces and rebellious children because the minister isn't home or too busy. Your spouse doesn't want the preacher at home, but they want you. Your children don't want the famous evangelist, but they need you.

2. Pray

The enemy loves to divide families. A house divided against itself can't stand (Mark 3:25). Husbands and wives must pray together. Then they must pray with their children. Even though there is a physical bond, a spiritual one must be formed because it's one of strength. Godly soul ties must be established so no matter what the enemy tries to do, families can fight for each other no matter what. Children need to learn how to operate in the supernatural so they can know that they have authority over the devil. When you train up a child in the way they should go, when they get older they will not depart from that way (Proverbs 22:6). A family that prays together stays together. Pray with your family, so the enemy is cast out of your home.

CHAPTER 6

Ministry

BY KIMBERLY MOSES

I NEVER THOUGHT THAT I would be a minister of the gospel, but God said otherwise. I learned that people come and go. Some are only around you because of the anointing and to get what they can. When they feel like they can't get anything else from you, then they are on to the next person. Others are around you but very fragile. When they are corrected or a disagreement happens, they get offended, block you on social or their phones, and never speak to you again. Rarely do you have some that will stay with you for the long haul. Some feel like they have outgrown you and start to get prideful and dishonor the anointing upon your life. Some people get too common and want to be your friend.

When some people see me and watch the vlogs that my husband and I do, they feel like they can pick up the phone and talk with me for hours. They don't understand the workload that God has given me and that talking two to three hours on the phone is not feasible because I would never be able to complete my ministry and business assignments. One day this lady emailed me and begged to talk with me over the phone. After weeks of her contacting me, I agreed. Once on the phone, I quickly realized that she didn't want anything. She didn't want ministry and wanted to talk about her life story. The next thing I knew, almost two hours had passed and I got behind on my work. She called me every day for weeks after and I didn't answer. She took the hint and stopped calling eventually.

Then there are times when people can't handle your humanity. They feel that you can't watch a movie with your family or have a life outside of ministry because you are a minister. If you get sad or tired from the warfare, they look at you as weak. One lady got too close to me and she went from wanting to be mentored to be a friend. I realized that not everyone is mature enough to handle your burdens or the challenges that arise. We must pray to see who to choose to be our armor-bearers or who God wants to be around us in ministry. I even learned to ask God who to help build or promote.

I have gotten hurt numerous times by those who were the most vocal about their support of the ministry. There was a lady who would always brag on me on social media and when we would speak, she would try to suck up to me. She would buy me gifts even after I asked her not to do so. She was very demonized and on my honeymoon, she kept calling for prayer. I grew to love and care for her deeply. One day, she cut me off and everyone connected to me. We were all worried and hurt by her actions. We truly had no idea what we did. I realize that the enemy will turn people against you without a valid reason. People loved Jesus one day when He was working miracles. When He was at His lowest moments, the same people shouted crucify him and chose Barabbas over him (Matthew 27:15-26).

We can't be flattered by compliments or get in pride when people come rubbing our egos. We must discern people's motives and why they want to connect with us. Some are mesmerized by the anointing but don't realize that there is a price that must be paid to walk in it. Some are jealous and can't transition with you when God shifts you into another season. They are used to you being on one level and when God starts to elevate you, they will fall off. In one season, God changed my whole circle and replaced them with new people.

WISDOM

1. Set boundaries

Boundaries must be set so things can be orderly in ministry. I don't allow my mentees to call me by my first name, but they must use my title. We aren't friends and if they get too common, they won't receive from me anymore. Also, they need to honor the anointing on my life. I also don't allow people to message me late at night unless it's an emergency because it's disrespectful. I have a family and got to wake up early each morning for prayer. I don't allow gossip and shut it down.

2. Establish your relationship

When people connect with me, the first thing that I do is establish our relationship. Am I your mentor, friend, or peer? If the relationship isn't established, then it's easy to get offended or have unrealistic expectations. People will know what to ex-

pect from me as a mentor or the mentor-mentee relationship. I will also know what to expect from them in return.

3. They belong to God

People come and go in ministry. When someone wants to leave your ministry, then let them go. I used to beg people to stay connected to me, but when someone has a mind that's made up, there is no stopping them from doing what they want to do. We must bless them and keep it moving. God will send the right people to help and support you on this journey. You don't want to get into witchcraft by praying against or cursing people that leave your ministry.

4. Pray for deliverance

Leaders need deliverance too. Deliverance is the children's bread. We must release the hurt, disappointments, and frustrations unto God so He can set us free. After we finish ministering to others, we must get before the Lord to cast our cares. So many leaders are bleeding behind the pulpit or walking around wounded because they are hurting. I will never forget the first time I saw a leader purge in front of the congregation. Witnessing that stressed the importance of our need for deliverance regardless of our positions.

5. Put your feeling on the back burner

When you are sick, tired, or don't feel like serving, you still have to serve because ministers are a bondservant to Christ

(Romans 1:1). You must love your Judas when you know who they are and what they are planning to do. You have to pray for your enemies and those that despitefully use you (Matthew 5:44). We have to guard our hearts because out of it flows the issues of life (Proverbs 4:23).

6. They will treat you the same as previous leaders

If they left the previous leaders wrong, then they will leave you wrong. For a season, the Lord showed me this valuable lesson. A few women wanted to connect with me, but they left their old leaders and dishonored them. They said their old leaders were witches, but the truth was these women were rebellious, had a vagabond spirit, and didn't want to submit to leadership. I am cautious about allowing these people to connect with me because they have a bad track record.

CHAPTER 7

Reconciliation

BY IRWIN "BUG" AND LESLIE HARVEY

According to the Oxford dictionary, reconciliation is defined as reuniting, bringing back together, reunion, and coming in agreement.[3] The Bible defines reconciliation as the restoration of friendly relations. Reconciliation involves a change in the relationship between God and man. Relationships have the ability to change from a state of hostility and destruction to one of agreement and companionship.[4]

"Therefore, if anyone is in Christ, they are a new creation: old things are passed away; behold, all things are made new. And all this by God, who reconciled us to himself by Jesus Christ, and gave us the ministry of reconciliation." (2 Corinthians 5:17-18 Jubilee Bible 2000)

The fact that we needed reconciliation means that our <u>relationship with God was broken</u>. Since God is Holy, we were the

---

[3]. "Reciliation defines as reuniting, bringing back together, reunion, coming into agreement" oxford dictionaries, Copyright © 2021 Oxford University Press".

[4]. https://www.biblestudytools.com/topical-verses/bible-verses-about-reconciliation".

ones to blame. God has forgiven us and still loves us when we were in our backslidden and worldly ways. Therefore, we must forgive. "Even if that person wrongs you seven times a day and each time turns again and asks forgiveness, you must forgive (Luke 17:4 NLT)." Forgiveness is a necessity.

The Holy Spirit presented these Scriptures on how God has reconciled with us through His Son Jesus Christ, who carried our sins on the cross. We all have sinned and fallen short, but praise be to God for His unmerited grace and mercy. When you are reconcilable, you must forgive; the two go hand in hand. I know it is not easy, but if we believe the Word of God, then we must act on it. How many times has God forgiven us? How many chances have we been granted? If it was not for His grace, there is no telling where I would be. I give God the glory.

LESLIE'S STORY

My husband and I were dating and we broke up after eighteen months, as stated in the previous chapter. Now, after nine months of being apart, I began to receive emails with his picture attached, phone calls, text messages, and voice messages were left on the cell and home phone. Can you imagine what I was feeling? After all this time, he broke up with me, and now he wants to talk. I was all in my emotions, and the anger arose, along with the pain, the embarrassment, and the shame. I ignored all of his messages. I asked myself how he had the audacity to try and contact me after all of this time. I was currently in another relationship at this time. This relationship was meaningless and just passing the time. A word of advice: Never leave one relationship without healing from your previous relationship. Healing is vital and absolutely necessary, so you can avoid making the same error again.

The man I was dating at the time was ready for marriage and told me he could not move forward because I still had feelings from my previous relationship. I disagreed entirely even though he saw right through me.

The last call from Bug stated: "If you do not return my call, I will come to your house and wait for you." I returned the call and agreed to meet him. Remember, I had not seen him in nine months and had no idea of what he wanted to discuss.

When I arrived at the restaurant, he was already there waiting and I sent him an unfriendly greeting. I was still upset, so seeing him face-to-face brought back so many unanswered questions and mixed emotions began to resurface.

He apologized for hurting me and told me he recognized I was wife material, but I was afraid to commit at the time. He appeared to be so sincere. I did not discern that he was lying. He was open and honest to all of the questions that I presented him. At that moment, I realized that I still loved him.

I was angry, bitter, and furious. I had to learn how to forgive and it was a process even after the proposal, which I accepted. The forgiveness of the past breaking-up, disappointments, and moving forward was a decision I had to make. If I had not have forgiven him, I would not be here. I am now married, enjoying my heart's desires with the life God has promised me.

BUG STORY

My brother Robert asked me about Leslie and I told him we were not together. He said that she is a good woman. I was not in a relationship, so I made several attempts to contact her and she did not respond at all. I had my co-worker Doris call Leslie immediately and Leslie answered her call. I went into my office and contacted her; she did not answer me. I left her a voice message demanding I would show up at her house if she did not return my call. Two weeks later, she accepted my call and agreed to meet me at a restaurant of her choice.

We went to Pappas Seafood and had a conversation about reconciliation. Leslie told me she was dating someone else and I replied that I would wait for her as long as the earth turned. She agreed to end the relationship to pursue her true love: me. Shortly after, I proposed to her and she accepted. We informed our families about our reconciliation and we set a wedding date shortly after. I have learned reconciliation and forgiveness go together; one cannot function without the other. We have learned so much from this and want to share the experience with others in order to prevent this from happening to them.

CHAPTER 8

Restoration

BY KEIMA SHANTAY SINCLAIR

True Love Is Worth Waiting For: Healing From a Toxic Marriage and Father/Daughter Relationship And Restoration

I AM A WOMAN WHO God inspired to share my story and focus on my unequally yoked relationship before, during, and after marriage. I am a divorcee of 13 years and a mother. My story is birthed from my pain of over 20 years being deceived into thinking to believe what real love is supposed to be like. It was only when I drew closer to the Heavenly Father God and began a prayer life that He blessed me with wisdom to know the difference between a carnal and a Spirit-filled life. If my life now is hidden in Christ, then I don't want to receive anything that opposes the Word of God and is contrary to His ways for my purpose on earth. Through my lessons, I've learned by adhering God's principles for my relationships. I hope I'll encourage you to put God first and always seek His wisdom for your relationship.

If you are not married yet, you can see what it is to trust God and be blessed to have discernment, insight, and confirmation from Him concerning your future spouse. You will know that it is best to depend on God and trust Him in all things. He does things just right in His own "perfect" time for our lives, so we should learn to wait on Father God. Getting married to the person that God did not choose can greatly affect us and those around us in ways we could have never imagined. It can also delay what God has in store for us or could cost us our lives. Proverbs 14:12 says, "There is a way that seems right unto man (mankind), but at the end thereof is death." So the end of that way or path is destructive and it's a way that leads to death.

I took a journey in my life that was simply not purposed for me by my Heavenly Father God to take. I went down a path that I have regretted as I reaped the consequences of my decisions. So, I have learned to trust God and experienced His amazing mercy, forgiveness, and grace, which helped to sustain me through taking a bad turn in my life that I should have never taken. God is so faithful. I have got to know God more than I ever have in my sufferings. I am to be able to share His love, grace, and mercy. God has brought me through many difficult and rough times due to my poor decision-making and being fooled by trickery concerning relationships. He can deliver and guide anyone with His wisdom and saving strength. He heals us through His precious Son, Jesus Christ. Through it all, I am grateful for God's grace, mercy, and having His hand on my life.

I must thank God also for the faithful and dedicated prayers of my grandmother, Mable Esther B. Thomas.

Growing up in a single-parent home, my mother taught me right from wrong. Yet, sometimes I just felt as if I wanted to do whatever I wanted to do and did not care what punishment was given to me by my mother. Although my parents were married, they were separated and not together. So, I did not have an example of parents having a strong commitment to each other. However, my grandparents carried that legacy that I could see and it was a blessing in my life. To date, I wish I could say that I modeled that faithfulness, love, strength, and bond that they had in my own marital relationship.

I was shy and super friendly. I did not know this then, but I was gullible and vulnerable to the point where I would let almost anyone from school and in my neighborhood(s) who'd said they like me and want to be my friend just freely walk into my life and I'll simply embrace them. It turned out I would follow them and the impact that decision made in my life I ended up copying some of their ways and behaviors.

Be not deceived: evil communications corrupt good manners. – 1 Corinthians 15:33

If the blind lead the blind, they both fall into the ditch.– Matthew 15:14

I became foolish in my thought process, planning and adhering to foolery and being with the wrong people. I had developed an attitude and had become disrespectful to my mother. My mother tried to shield and protect me to the best of her ability, but sometimes I did not care to listen to her. One day she made a phone call to my dad as she thought he could help talk some good sense into me and give sound instruction and share some wisdom. She expected my dad to explain to me that I was too young to have a boyfriend, but he let my mom and I both know that it was fine. He felt that it was okay for me to have a boyfriend because he didn't see anything wrong. So, of course, I saw that they couldn't agree, and I simply went with my dad's opinion and used that as permission to date without knowing about true, sincere, and purposeful courtship.

A door was opened less than a year later, and an older guy took an interest in me and commanded that I be his girlfriend. Before I knew it he had pressured me into being intimate with him and I had gotten pregnant. He was happy and I was confused. I would become a single-parent with a baby out of wedlock, having no employment and have not completed my High School education and living with my mother and my younger siblings. I heard a soft, gentle voice to keep my baby. (I know now that my grandmother was praying for my unborn baby and me). And so, I did not get an abortion, although some adults in my life had their opinions thinking that I should get one. I realized that I had embarrassed my mother because I heard her say how I was too young to have a baby and she is not ready to become a grandmother because she was too young. She also felt like she was not finished raising my siblings and me. I really couldn't make much sense of any of it then. Nevertheless, my mother accepted this sudden shock and embraced me with love and cared for me during my pregnancy and when my first baby was born. I prayed to God to bless my baby to be a boy and my heart's desires were answered. My mother had moved us to the south of North Jersey for a better environment, so my siblings would not experience what happened to me. Unfortunately, unlearned "boys" and "men" with their selfish intentions are everywhere.

I had some "boyfriends," which were immature relationships and a waste of my time because what they thought and wanted to share with me, such as their time, love, and themselves ended with me being an experiment. As I got in my early twenties, I no longer wanted to be just some guy's experiment to see if I could be the one for him. But I really desired a true, sincere, and purposeful relationship. I wanted somebody to love me and to love them in return. If he loves me, he will love and accept my son. My oldest son lost his father when he was a young boy. He hadn't had a lot of time with him before his passing. This experience was very hard on him, but he cherishes the times he did have with his father. So, the man I desired was to be family-oriented.

I thought I was doing the right things concerning my relationship between my fiancé and me. I met him one evening by sneaking off away from my dear cousin's side and later found out that he was the uncle to my cousin's child. One day, I shared some things with my mom about how they talked, yelled, and treated one another at their house when I visited with my cousin. So, my mother said I had no business going over there and she instructed me not to go back to their house with my cousin.

My mother expressed over and over her concerns for her children. She doesn't just let us go over or spend a night at anybody's house because she didn't know everything about them, and anything can happen. Especially if she personally doesn't know that family, she'd rather keep me safe because she knows how we should be cared for and raised. Needless to say, I rejected her instruction and was very upset at her saying things I later regretted. My mom noticed the difference in how I was changing and developing an attitude with her when I would go into that atmosphere and come back home. I did not tell my cousin what my mom had said. I found ways and excuses to go back there with her to see my fiancé again and he liked that also. It was the attention he gave to me and places he'd promised to take me. He told me we could probably live together someday, and I really liked that. I thought that it was so sweet of him to share those caring words with me, although he was a bit hardcore and bad with his mouth when he spoke.

I recall my mom telling me to watch a man and how he treats his mother, because that is how he will treat me. Another time she would say, "If a person shows you who they are, believe them because that man is letting you know who he is and what he is about." I found this to be true because I observed his relationship with his mother. Even in some conversations we had while reminiscing on our past relationships, he would tell me how he had his way and dealt with his ex-girlfriend of five years and with other ex-girlfriends. This was an eye-opener, red flag, and a warning for me, but I did not take heed to walk away from him. I made an excuse, believing that our past experiences were our past and this was our present. I thought it was up to us to better our future than those relationship experiences. But deep down in my heart, I knew that I deserved and wanted better. Yet, I chose to commit to him regardless. There was another time I remembered what my mom taught me that if a boy says he likes me, he will wait for me and will not want to get me in the bed with him right away to have sex with me. Also, he can get me pregnant or give me a disease. She said, the right young man would ask if he can meet my parents, asking their permission to court me. I pondered what my mom was discussing with me, but I did not completely understand it all. I did not listen and ended up buying into the guy's games and lies.

The same guy that my mom could not see me being with became my fiancé. My mom knew who I get myself involved in a relationship matters because it is very important what type of person I allow in my life. I did not tell my mom, but I knew my fiancé carried deep past issues of emotional wounds, shutting people out of his life, and holding onto grudges, unforgiveness, and bitterness. Unfortunately, drinking alcohol, smoking cigarettes habitually and marijuana and pornographic stuff was what he turned to soothe and cope. His biological dad was not stable in his life growing up and he had indifferences. He experienced relationship difficulties with his mother that he had buried so deep. My prayers to date: Heavenly Father, in Christ Jesus' name, I pray that he let's go of his concealed past discouragements, disappointments, failures, hurt and crises and whatever else he is going through that You only know of. I believe you, Lord, that he will have the strength to surrender it all to you, Lord, for his liberation and salvation. Lord, I pray that he never pursues vengeance or retaliation when he gets irate towards me, our children or takes it out on someone else. Father God let his heart, family, love, and trust be completely healed and re-established in Christ Jesus' name. Amen.

" A wise son maketh a glad father: but a foolish son is the heaviness of his mother." –Proverbs 10:1

I knew at a young age that I would serve God for the rest of my life. Regardless of what I knew about my fiancé and his past and the things untold, he knew what I faced in inappropriate situations as a young teen. I believed in my mind I could marry whomever I desired and take him on my God-given journey to reach our destiny together. I had talked to God and let Him know that I planned to read the Bible more often and go to church more persistently, read together, study, and we will follow God's will as one. But there was constant resistance and rejection on my fiancé's part. I just didn't understand why. So, I decided to wait and believed that I just needed to have patience until he was ready because I didn't want to pressure him. I really could not share Christ or have godly conversations with him because each time I tried to, he had expressed little interest. I was a babe in Christ and recently had rededicated my life to God. What a faithful friend I have in Jesus Christ!

Hear instruction, and be wise, and refuse it not. Blessed is the man that heareth Me,...For whoso findeth Me findeth life, and shall obtain favour of the Lord. But he that sinneth against Me wrongeth his own soul:... –Proverbs 8:33-36

The fear of the Lord is the beginning of wisdom: and the knowledge of the holy is understanding. –Proverbs 9:10

WORKING ON PUTTING GOD BACK IN FIRST PLACE!

But seek ye first the kingdom of God, and his righteousness; and all these things shall be added unto you. –Matthew 6:33

During my early twenties, I continued to put my fiancé before God, myself, and everyone else in my life. At some point, I knew this practice that was okay with my fiancé was dysfunctional and out of order. However, I allowed myself to be in such a position to deal with verbal abuse, some physical mistreatment and control for years. Yet, realizing it was unhealthy for my son to grow up seeing these things. But I kept this matter on the back burner and decided to move forward in this relationship, figuring things would work itself out in time and get better for "our family." After a while, I had enough and showed my mom while talking to her one day. We were sitting inside a vehicle and I let her know what my fiancé had done to the side of my face. I told her that I was leaving and she agreed. She was happy for me for taking a stand and making the right choice to part ways with him. My mom told me that he was not good for me for the first, second and third time. So, I packed all my things and moved my son and I out of that toxic situation. My son was about six years old at the time. He seemed to be very happy and relieved too.

Unfortunately, a few weeks after moving out my ex-fiancé's place, he started calling me to apologize, and persuaded me to return to him. His entire conversation centered on him reminding me of the fun and good times we had shared. He went on telling me how much he loves and misses his family. I ignored him for a little while and then I was convinced that he might want to do right this time because he had time to see what he missed. Wrong! I made the foolish decision to go back to him and when I let my mother know, it grieved her heart. I was eager to see if he had changed his ways. I thought to myself, I rather not live back with my mom but be on my own because I am a grown woman.

On a partly sunny summer day, I visited with family at my grandparent's house, where I had seen my cousin at the front gate. This is the same dearest cousin through whom I met my fiancé. She has a powerful testimony of what God has done for her after having had failed 'boyfriend and girlfriend' relationships. She has been blessed to be married to a man who God told she was his wife. Praise the Lord! And over 20 years, they are still married! My cousin was newly married at the time. She was encouraging me by explaining how it is right to be married and it is good in God's eyes. For some reason, I thought to myself I had better listen closely to what she is saying because she seemed so happy, settled, and content. Then she proceeded to declare a Scripture saying, "In the Bible, it says it is better to marry than to burn." I let her know that I did not know that and said I would talk to my fiancé because this is serious, and I was afraid of burning in Hell for fornication. So, I hurried to talk with my fiancé, and he agreed that we should get married sooner rather than later. And so, I made plans to find a pastor to marry us. My fiance said he knew someone whose life had changed after he became a minister. He agreed to talk to him. The minister got back to him and agreed to marry us. But first, we had to commit to counseling sessions.

At our first counseling session, the minister asked us the same questions. He saw that we were prematurely deciding to get married and told us we were not ready and needed to attend more counseling sessions. This upset me because I believed that it did not take all of that. I could not accept his advice or sound counsel concerning our soon-to-be union in marriage. So, I called him the next day and told him if he would marry us in the next few days, I would pay him double, and in seconds he had agreed. Well, we never made it to our second or third counseling sessions because I was in such a hurry and was holding off, the best I could, on being intimate until we eloped so that I could please God. I was afraid of going to hell if I was tempted to sleep with him another day without being married.

I had let a few people know what I had planned on doing just a day or two in advance. My mom didn't agree with this plan. I also had another cousin tell me if I married him that my kids would come out ugly. I believed it was her way, back then, of scaring me not to make such a life-long foolish decision. I was hurt and upset that she said that, but I said to myself, "They are just haters and do not want to see me happy."

One of my favorite aunts, who has amazing spiritual gifts of visions and prophecy, etc., came from out of state to visit our loved ones. While sitting at my grandparent's kitchen table, she sat across from me, smiling and talking. Then suddenly saying,

"God said whatever you are about to do, don't do it. He has somebody for you." I was stunned, asking myself, how does she know that I am getting married tomorrow. I gave what she said very little thought and still decided that I would be with my fiancé. I thought, "I do not even know who God has for me, but I know this man I am with right now (so I thought), and we have been together, on and off, in our relationship for many years. Plus, the fact that we shared the same family." My little second cousin was his nephew. We imagined when we would become married, we would be uncle and aunt to him – thinking that was so adorable and cute.

On the very day of our very small, intimate, casual wedding ceremony in 1999, I was very nervous. Even on that special day, I tolerated being verbally abused and was just hoping that he would change his disrespectful ways towards me after we were married. We were in the gazebo in the park, where we agreed to tie the knot. Suddenly, when everyone got into position, I was shown a vision of me running to my car that will save me from making a huge mistake. I ignored that vision and decided to stay focused on marrying my fiancé. I still felt uneasy about whether to go through with marrying him. I saw a vision in Heaven of extreme sadness for me and one large teardrop falling from the Lord in the sky. This was very unusual for me to see something like that.

When the minister reached the part of the vows for me to respond: {I do.} "[Bride], do you take [the Groom] to be your wedded husband to live together in marriage? Do you promise to love him, comfort him, honor and keep him for better or worse, for richer or poorer, in sickness and health and forsaking all others, be faithful only to him so long as you both shall live?" I instantly heard a serious voice sounding like rushing waters saying, "NO"! So, with my hands inside of my fiancé's hands, I was at a standstill and I hesitated. I looked around and said, "Who said that?" But everyone seemed clueless to even know what I was referring to or talking about.

It was days later, after having declared "I do" for marriage in front of a small gathering in the park of six people, including my young son, I was miserable. I realized that I should not have gotten married to my fiancé because I had realized that it was God telling me "No." I felt very sorrowful and apologetic. With that, I gave a call to the minister who married us to ask him not to send in the paperwork to the Vital Statistics marriage department. He told me it was too late. I am married and he had already sent the papers off in the mail. I was thinking to myself, "What have I just done?" I couldn't even turn back to undo what I have done; in the name of Father, Son and Holy Spirit and witnesses, I have solemnly vowed those vows and said, "I do." I knew then I had made a very serious commitment.

I wish I had known with Spiritual understanding to take that word of encouragement from my dearest cousin. I knew my cousin meant well by sharing Scripture with me. However, I wish that I would have taken it before the Lord in prayer. I should have told my cousin that I would pray about it to see what the Lord would have me to do. I was not mature enough to completely understand spiritually the things God has protected me from. One act of obedience from the very beginning would put me on the right path. Only if I had heeded the earlier counsel and the people God has brought into my life to encourage me to make the right decisions I would have avoided the pitfall of being involved in the wrong relationships for me and my son's life. A relationship approved by God means everything.

If any of you lack wisdom, let him ask of God, that giveth to all men liberally, and upbraideth not; and it shall be given him. –James 1:5

The fear of the Lord is the beginning of knowledge; fools despise wisdom and instruction. –Proverbs 1:7

The wisdom of the prudent is to discern his way, but the folly of fools is deceiving. –Proverbs 14:8

THE ATTACKS AND UP & DOWN EMOTIONS

Growing up, I would hear in my household, "If you make your bed hard, you have to lay in it." Proverbs Chapter 1 describes God trying to refocus the Babylonians after being led astray as they were not listening and obeying Him. They turned to listen to others with the worldly influence of power in their lives. They refused God's counsel after counsel and reproof. So, God let them go to choose their way. I can relate because I suffered being unequally yoked under a vowed covenant. I was extremely devastated in my marriage, wondering to myself at one time: "How could one decision, one choice seemed to delay and ruin my whole life?" I also got very angry with God and said, "Lord, I said I was sorry for disobeying your warning

of protection and instructions for my life. Why am I still being punished? Why am I a slave to my decision I made for my life many years ago? You wanted me to forgive. I did that. You want me to forgive myself and forget what was behind me, and I gave my marriage problems to You Lord." When my husband triggered me, I admit I would take it all back again and put it in my hands to deal with it my way, only to find out later the situation did not always go the way I thought it should go or the way that I wanted it to turn out. I further told the Lord, I realized now that what was going on in our relationship before we got married would only be magnified in my marriage, especially because we were not equally yoked nor on one accord in God.

I was confessing and praying Scriptures for my husband's salvation and for God to bless our union. It was from marriage counseling with our Bishop, which he refused to keep going and did not take his visits seriously to help our marriage. I consulted with other women and men of God to pray for us. I went on to fasting, praying, and putting anointing oil in his shoes and on his pillow. Also, I had an evangelist visit and anointed our home and to discuss our marriage. Things got better with his attitude and every now and then, I saw things happen with him that I know it only had to be God making him do right by me. But he still refused to surrender his life to Christ. Instead, he cursed God. So, I began to pray that God would forgive him because he didn't know what he was doing. I began sending in my prayer requests to the deliverance ministries I was connected to and sowing seeds. I prayed the prayers that will help break the strongholds of the powers of darkness, idol worship, witchcraft, voodoo, hex, and sorcery spirits that some people down his family line and generations going back have dabbled in. Then my husband would talk about he might start going to church with us again, but he kept going back on his word. I know that the enemy, the devil, didn't want to let him go. He has no choice because God's Word has been spoken over his life. And so, he would remain angry and get angrier. Our prayers are not in vain and we left his salvation to God. I believe with all my heart, God will save him before he leaves this world because the prayers of the saints of God avails much.

Hatred stirreth up strifes: but love covereth all sins. – Proverbs 10:12

There were times where I would slip into a state of depression where I was so miserable and devastated in my marriage. I thought, "Why am I here with this man putting up with him? If I am gone, I would be released forever from the man I should have not married." On the other hand, I did not want to go to hell nor be forever separated from the Heavenly Father if I brought any kind of harm to myself as this could be very painful for my children. They need me to help raise them in God's love and His ways because their dad won't. He doesn't know how unless he gave his heart to Christ.

God delivered me from any thinking that did not line up with His promises for my life. With that, I had the victory. God has always sent someone right in the niche of time, whether by hearing a sermon, a prayer on television, receiving a phone call, or someone visits me in person to speak life unto me to save me. There was a word of encouragement to restore me.

The saying goes, "God's not through with me yet!" I still have a great work for Him to do on earth for my purpose and destiny. I am aware now that God uses my story to help heal, deliver, and set others free. That is why I am still here in my right mind, well and alive. Thank you, dear Lord, for saving me through all those discouraging and very difficult times I have faced. Your power is greater than anything I have gone through. Your love is everlasting. Your grace is sufficient for your children! Thank you, Lord.

One day I called my mom, discussing with her my problems I faced with my husband. I planned to come back home. She responded, "You are married now. Let your husband take care of you and those children." It frustrated me to hear this, but she was right. However, since I did not want to fully digest this truth, I was sad and felt rejected and alone. But the Lord always made a way to show His amazing love for me. I would get out of that pity party and instead keep my eyes and mind focused on Him. In no time at all, I had a perfect peace that caused my focus to shift to God's promises and the important things concerning my children and me and their future.

There is a way which seemeth right to a man (mankind), but the end thereof are the ways of death.– Proverbs 14: 12 (In other words, you'll find out in the end that you took a road to destruction.)

Marriage is honourable in all, and the bed undefiled: but whoremongers and adulterers God will judge. –Hebrews 13:4

Restoration

Thou wilt keep him in perfect peace, whose mind is stayed on thee: because he trusteth in thee. –Isaiah 26:3

If Heavenly Father God gave me a breakthrough that I needed in my life, He could do the very same for you. He's always on time and His timing is perfect. The pain and the years of hurt that I have suffered from being lonely and raising my children pretty much on my own in my marriage and being misunderstood, self-will and self-pleasing, and as damaging my decisions were, I yet believed God would be with me through it all. Even when I turned my back on God, He has never left my side.

And I give unto them eternal life; and they shall never perish, neither shall any man pluck them out of my hand. – John 10:28

Let your conversation be without covetousness; and be content with such things as ye have: for He hath said, I will never leave thee, nor forsake thee. –Hebrews 13:5

Nay, in all these things we are more than conquerors through Him that loved us. – Romans 8:37

~We can do all things through Christ Jesus, which strengthens us. – Philippians 4:13

GOD IS FAITHFUL

But without faith it is impossible to please him: for he that cometh to God must believe that he is, and that he is a rewarder of them that diligently seek him. – Hebrews 11:6

I had eight years of marriage with a man that God did not choose for me. It was beyond challenging that I have faced due to me being unequally yoked. I remember a season where I was heavily weeping before God, fasting and praying to Him to deliver me from this marriage at once. I told God I was so sorry that I disobeyed Him and got married to this person. Still weeping, I made a vow to the Lord, "If You get me out of this marriage, and You give me another chance, I will follow Your ways regarding marriage and I will do things right the next time. Plus, there was adultery committed in my marriage." About a week later, an Evangelist called me and prophesied, "God says He has granted your divorce. He said, "He has tried your husband's heart and he told him, no. He doesn't want to change."

I was extremely grateful, relieved, and elated that I was going to be free. I didn't know how or when it would be done, but I held on to this promise from God with all my heart and soul. When the time came, I was quickened in my spirit to act on the divorce process immediately. My husband put up a fight and even told me, "You will never leave me. You belong to me, forever." It was getting close to the deadline of when he had to execute the documents and my husband kept refusing to go with me to sign and notarize our divorce papers. My attorney told me it was getting close to the time and if he didn't sign, I would have to start the process all over again. I started to be very concerned and cried out to God again for victory because I was probably not going to see that lump sum of money that I received like that for a while as a full-time housewife. I could not help but to think about how the timing was perfect and how everything just lined itself up for my freedom and submission to him as his wife. Through this trying time, I still held on to God's promises that no matter what it looked like, I was going to get a divorce. I kept believing and reciting in my spirit what God has already declared. This gave me the faith I needed to hold on. It was not simple because it was a spiritual war. I knew in my spirit the Heavenly Father would honor His promise and set me free.

One Saturday, my husband was off work and the Holy Spirit instructed me to get the children ready to proceed to get the papers signed and notarized. I felt a leap of hope within me. I followed God's instructions and moved in faith. My husband was busy doing other things, but I approached him when I felt led to let him know that we ought to head now to get the divorce papers signed and notarized. After that, I proceeded to go to my car with our children. Although he was disturbed by me letting him know this, angry, threatened, and cursed the children and me out, he got into his truck and led the way to our destination. God had moved on my husband's heart and he signed the papers. God gave me the victory! Everything had come to fruition and God's perfect will was established concerning my heart's desire.

Sometime later, after my divorce, God has been faithful to save me from remarrying my ex-husband not only once but twice! Once when I was still living in our house with my ex-husband while the paperwork was being processed for divorce, he had expressed that we should go to the Justice of Peace at our City Hall to get married again because he believes that we should not be getting a divorce. I was feeling the moment and said I would love to give him a second chance. He was spending time with us being family-oriented, etc. However, when I saw how he was still in his ways and not putting God first and getting to know Him, I let him know. He looked down with sadness or remorse and said he knows. I told him that it would not work, and he understood that, so we went back to our separate spaces in the house.

The second time my ex-husband proposed to me was when I was living at my parent's dwelling and we were on our way back from visiting my old neighborhood in New York. He surprised me and presented me with a beautiful diamond ring and, with that, expressed to me how much he loved me and missed our family together. I was surely in awe hearing his words and sincerity. But then I felt my help from the Lord coming on to help me stand tall, firm, and be strong and courageous to politely decline his offer once again.

Have not I commanded thee? Be strong and of a good courage; be not afraid, neither be thou dismayed: for the LORD thy God is with thee whithersoever thou goest. – Joshua 1:9

MIRACULOUS FAMILY RESTORATION AND DADDY COMING TO THE RESCUE

And Jesus looking upon them saith, With men it is impossible, but not with God: for with God all things are possible.– Mark 10:27

For with God nothing shall be impossible. –Luke 1:37

Since my marriage, I thought if my biological dad were present, things would be different. He could have led and encouraged me to have heeded to his discipline and not go down a path with a man that God did not choose for my life. Although I haven't spoken to my father about how I feel about him being absent, I talked to him from my heart out loud in private, knowing he could not hear me. But God hears me, and He knows my dad.

Thoughts of the heart to my dad: I have a Heavenly Father who loves me even when you didn't. He is more than enough and because of Him, I forgave you. When you weren't there for me, He was there. God blessed me and brought my dearest uncles into my life, who I have drawn close to and they were good mentors to me. One day, I told one of my uncle's sons that his father has been like a father and blessed my children and me. I have wasted too much time pondering and crying my heart out. Every now and then, I get frustrated because a father is supposed to be a teacher, protector, and provider. Then I wonder if my life would have been better and my relationship would have flourished and succeeded if he was in my life right there by my side.

There is too much deep hurt and devastation from fatherlessness that brings upon children. Fathers must step up to their true position and roles and have accountability to God to love, discipline, and have a good influence in their child's life. To be not only present, but visual to teach a child to be responsible and productive young men and women in society. I had to reach an understanding. First, a man must get it right with God. Then he can make it right with his children. So, I got to a place where I am ready to be content and be thankful for the things I do have in my life. The rest of the things that I do not have control over and the pain of my father being absent, I released to God. I left it there for Him to work a miracle. This was my season of letting go and letting God handle it.

Then quite sometime after lifting my dad up to the Heavenly Father God in prayer, a woman of God prophesied to me declaring, "The Lord will bring my natural father back to me and until then he will have no peace until he makes it right with me, and in my next marriage there will not be a sting in my marriage." I was amazed, astonished, and believed the Word of the Lord. Almost two years later, I moved from Hudson Valley, NY, back to North Jersey. My mother was blessed to have seen and communicated with my father a couple of times. One of those times, he inquired about me. That was my first miracle God worked out. Hallelujah! My dad did not call me right away, but it was a dream come true and such a blessing just to hear his voice when he did call. It was a blessing to see how he had a relationship with God and a prayer life. There was an anointing on his life as he let God use him for His Glory. It was also glorious to witness how Father God has led my dad to get involved with street ministry and sharing Gospel tracts to people who are lost that need to come back to Jesus. I found that to be quite amazing because that is what I was also missioned to do.

My dad has gifts God bestowed upon his life to pray for people and share God's Word with them. The people he prays for God moves miraculously on their behalf and heals, delivers, or blesses them with the miracles they believed God for. He prays for me and I pray for him. We sometimes pray together. We bless each other with the things we may need. Most of all, I am so grateful for my dad taking the time to impart wisdom to us and teach my children about the things of God, which has been a blessing.

God's healing restoration has blessed me with feeling like I never had any missing or lost time with my natural father. Right away, my children connected with their grandpa. It was never a strange or boring moment being with my dad. Right when I needed his support for school matters with my children, he was there. Before all else, my dad got himself right with God first for his salvation and God prepared him for a relationship with me. Therefore, he knows how to love his grandchildren and me in Godly reverence. My dad had shared with me about the time he heard from God. He got out of that situation of living in sin and he walked away and never went back! Praise God for my dad's obedience to God! God's timing is so wonderful, and I was blessed to see the fruit of me trusting in my Heavenly Father.

I was in my late 30's when I gave my concerns in prayer to God. Around the age of 40, I received the prophetic Word about my dad. I started my relationship with my dad. My dad being in my children's lives is better than I could ever have imagined. When God does something, it is so marvelous in our eyes.

Now unto Him that is able to do exceedingly abundantly all we could ask or think according to the power which works in us...– Ephesians 3:20

The Lord will perfect that which concerneth me: thy mercy, O Lord, endureth for ever: forsake not the works of thine own hands.– Psalm 138:8

THE COUNTERFEITS

To date, in my 13 years as a divorcee, while I was seeking God for strength to practice celibacy until being sent the man that is right for my children and me, some temptations arose. Four different men showed their strong desire and interest in me, but it wasn't long that God revealed their true spirits, intentions, motives, and hidden secrets/lies. A few claimed to know God and we even went to church. I was asked by a few of them to remain in their lives as a friend because they did not want to let go (soul ties), but praise God I was strong enough in the Spirit to let them go completely. And so, Glory to God, those people were completely gone from out of my life. I really had to take a stand and let my yes be yes and my no, No! My dad being in my life now really is a blessing – it's never too late. God was able to show my dad a vision of a man coming into my life and when he came, the physical appearance was very similar to whom my dad described. My dad had one talk with him and confirmed that this man was not the man God has for me. Glory to God! After some time, my mom even let me know how she did not think he was the right man for me. God will show us things to come and bless us to know the difference as we trust Him. God will never lead us wrong; His ways are righteous and blessed.

I have sensed it was a cycle to trap or keep me bound in the same situations resulting in the same outcomes. A guy sees me and says they want to get to know me and wants me to be with them as their spouse. Either I can sense immediately that they are just talking with the wrong intentions concerning me to get what they want or it becomes a challenge and I am not completely sure about them. I do not want to misjudge their motive, so I would seek God in prayer, asking first who is this man? Lord, did you send him? Lord, I thank you for revealing to me what I need to know about this man. Heavenly Father God is faithful! What is hidden in the dark is brought forth to the light for me to see that their word is not their bond and not the Godly man for my children and me.

I had begun to seek God and pray differently concerning my next relationship. I have sincerely prayed for God to hide me from men's lustful or infatuated eyes, intent, motives, and

spirits they may have towards me. I refused to let the devil use them to distract me. Only let the man of God that You have for my children and me and for ministry have eyes to see me; and eyes for me only as his wife sent to by You Lord for him. God is so faithful! No man seemed to have noticed me at all in a very long time. God has even calmed and balanced my hormones that way, I am not sinning against Him with any sexual feelings, thoughts, or am tempted in any way that displeases the Lord. I praise God. My waiting season for a husband is pure and holy before Him! I thank the Lord because He made the body and knows exactly how to manage, heal, and bring the balance we need. But I said, "Lord, when my husband comes, I need my fire back for the bedroom," and I praise Him in advance because Father God is faithful.

It matters who I marry because I do not know a man's family bloodline and what happened in their generations, but God knows. He helped me in one relationship that I was starting to get into. I really like this man. One day I visited him at his apartment. He had asked me to help him look for something and I came into an Ouija Board. When I confronted him about it and let him know that he had to get rid of it, he expressed to me he can't because he is doing a project with it. I said, "If I am going to be here, and we are going to be together, I must tear it up and destroy it in Jesus Christ's name." He just stared at me strangely and immediately, I began tearing it up into pieces and stomping in it, pleading the Blood of Jesus Christ of Nazareth and taking it out of the apartment. He was furious but did not stop me. God is faithful to reveal hidden darkness that I do not voluntarily want in my life again.

The thief (Satan, the devil) cometh not, but for to steal, and kill and to destroy: I (Jesus Christ) am come that they might have life, and that they might have it more abundantly.– John 10:10

PUTTING GOD FIRST BEFORE BEING FOUND

Whoso findeth a wife findeth a good thing, and obtaineth favour of the Lord. – Proverbs 18:22

During my preparation for my future marriage and before I say I do, I often examine myself to make sure I am in alignment with the will of the Heavenly Father God in all my ways. I acknowledge Him being first in my life. That way, I will lovingly submit to my future husband because I desire to be equally yoked together with a man who loves God with all his heart, mind, and soul. If a man loves God, He will obey God and love me like Christ loves the Church and gave His life for us. I have learned to wait patiently on the Heavenly Father God and put my trust in Him for my future husband. I am praying for my future husband even before we meet face to face. I used to have a question in my mind: is there just one real mate (woman, wife) out there in the world for a man that he is supposed to find and marry? However, it is not so much about a man finding the right person for himself in as much as it is becoming the person the Heavenly Father made him to be. We are blessed when we keep God's ways. He knows what's best for our lives better than we do! God created us. It's not the other way around.

Now therefore hearken unto me, O ye children: for blessed are they that keep my ways. – Proverbs 8:32

Forgive one another as quickly and thoroughly as God in Christ forgave you. – Ephesians 4:32~

Whether you are married to the right person that was joined together by God or to the wrong person where you did not go before God first in prayer concerning this person, marriage is a gift from God and regardless, He honors marriage. So, please continue to seek the Lord concerning the things you are going through in your marriage and let His Holy Spirit lead you. Read the Bible and search the Scriptures. Decree and declare God's Word over your marriage. Find a powerful, deliverance prayer line such as Prophetess Kimberly Moses, where you can also receive sound prophetic counsel, insight, and prayer for marriages. Find other positive support of good influence that you may need. There are so many blessed testimonies from married couples experiencing God's miracles in their marriages. These testimonies can help strengthen your faith to stand on God's Word for your marriage and for a miraculous and glorious turnaround from the Lord, too.

Wives ought to stay strong in the ways of the Lord and keep praying and fasting for their husband or wife. Believe God to turn around your situation in your favor according to His will and magnificent glory.

Where no counsel is, the people fall: but in the multitude of counsellors there is safety. –Proverbs 11:14

Restoration

He healeth the broken in heart, and bindeth up their wounds. – Psalm 147:3

Cast thy burden upon the Lord, and He shall sustain thee: He shall never suffer the righteous to be moved. –Psalm 55:22

Casting all your care upon Him; for He careth for you. – 1 Peter 5:7

My prayer in love to the single ladies is to continue to get closer to God and seek Him with all your heart, mind, and soul because He is your first love. He is your everything. You can pray for God to give you love for Him. This also prepares you to love your future husband the way God intended us to love our husbands. God is a good Father and He will never let us down. He will bring healing and comfort to heal your soul. He will restore and deliver you from any soul ties or old baggage from past relationships so it won't be poisonous to the new relationship with the person God has for you. Anytime, 24/7, He is available for you. Just call out to the God of your salvation in Christ Jesus's name. He is the ONE that will save you from despair, trouble and heartache. He is a faithful God and a promise keeper. If I seem like I am getting discouraged or feeling lonely, I ask the Lord to give me a fresh touch of His anointing. I am refreshed and strengthened to go on stronger. I am at peace because my mind is staying on Him. I am reminded of a Scripture that blesses me so much during my 'single waiting season.' Proverbs 13:12 says, "Hope deferred makes the heart sick: but when the desire comes, it is a tree of life." So, I would bounce right back to having hope again, knowing I am waiting on the Lord for the best man He has for me – this is glorious! Hallelujah! True and honorable love is worth the waiting.

My breakthrough came only when I humbled myself and quieted my spirit just enough to let go and let God do what only He can do; for God to be Lord and Savior in my life. We depend on Him to help and guide us in the way we should go daily because He is our everlasting Father. God wants His people to know His love, power, and grace. If you are consistently working things out in your own power, you will be unable to know His power and what He can do for you. I used to look for joy and happiness from a man in my relationship, but only God can make us whole. God wants us to be satisfied. But our joy and peace come from when we delight ourselves in Him for God to give us the desires of our hearts. Glory be to God!

If it is the will of Heavenly Father for your life, the Lord provides a woman for each man, but we must pray about it and wait on His provision to be revealed unto us. The Bible teaches about a prudent woman. A prude (honorable and worthy) woman is a good choice. She's not relatively inexpensive and unholy. She is a woman who waits for God to find her a mate and won't marry someone that doesn't share her beliefs and Christian values. She honors the Lord God's commands and pursues being equally yoked. (Ref. Proverbs 19:14, Proverbs 31, 2 Corinthians 6:14, Hebrews 13:4 KJV)

God lets us know in 1 Samuel 16:7 that he knows man. He does not see how we see him because we look at the outer appearance, but God looks on the heart. We want a person from God that is after the Lord's own heart. The man sent by Father God will value and see me how Father God understands me. We are marvelously and wonderfully made by our Father in Heaven. If the man is from the world (carnal-minded) and hasn't given his life to Christ for his salvation, he cannot love a woman the right way because He does not know God and the love of God. Most men do not know what it is to be a committed mate to a future wife. But they are out there, and God knows them by name. I should know this because my grandfather was one of those men, a fine committed man who loves God and his wife, family, and extended family with all his heart.

Before I remarry, I know that I belong to God first. I am married to Him and the love He bestows is for me to Himself and to love others. When we make a mistake and fall into temptation, we ought to cry out for God's help to get back up again and get back on the straight and narrow path of righteousness. When God commands us to flee from sexual immorality, He intends for us to stay pure and holy unto Him. Our body is the temple of the Holy Spirit where He dwells and we want to respect and honor God. When a person sins with sexual thoughts, imagination, and sexual impurity, the Holy Spirit is grieved. But the rich mercy and grace of the Lord is always right there for you to help restore you to purity. Be willing to repent and turn from that sexual sin and opt never to do it again. God will do the rest to keep you strong and from falling.

The Lord has blessed my life and strengthened me to be content and to trust and wait on Him. God the Father will keep you from deception and a big disaster in the path ahead, if you will listen to Him.

"I am the LORD who heals you." – Exodus 15:26

"Now unto him that is able to keep you from falling, and to present you faultless before the presence of His glory with exceeding joy, To the only wise God our Saviour, be glory and majesty, dominion and power, both now and ever. Amen." – Jude 1:24-25 ~

CHAPTER 9

In Sickness and In Health, Marriage & Ministry

BY ERIK AND CHRISTINA NELSON

3 John 2 says, "Beloved, I wish above all things that thou mayest prosper and be in health, even as thy soul prospereth."

This is our journey. How we met, and how God used us to help others just like us. We are a happily married couple who were both diagnosed with Multiple Sclerosis.

Multiple sclerosis (MS) is an autoimmune disease that affects the brain and spinal cord (central nervous system). MS is caused by damage to the myelin sheath. This sheath is the protective covering that surrounds nerve cells. When this nerve covering is damaged, nerve signals slow or stop. The nerve damage is caused by inflammation. Inflammation occurs when the body's own immune cells attack the nervous system. This can occur along any area of the brain, optic nerve, and spinal cord.

We're no different than any other married couple. We dated, courted, and got married on an unusually warm 67 degree day: on January 11, 2020. I felt that, that was God's approval. 67 degrees in January? The thing that makes us unique is that we both share the same diagnosis. With that, God brought us together for a purpose! This is our story.

ERIK'S STORY:

In August 2013, I was diagnosed with Multiple Sclerosis. I began to experience issues within my body. I, just like most men, ignore signs that something was going on with me. Why? Because I work out every day and I thought I was eating healthy. I started a push up challenge with myself where I wanted to do 1,000 push-ups a day. I finally worked up to 900 push-ups a day, so this particular day, it must have been in July of 2013. I was doing about 900 push-ups and just out of the blue, I fell on my face. My left hand had given away. It happened a second time and I knew something was wrong, so I decided to go to the emergency room. So while making several trips to the ER I was told to reach out to my Primary Care doctor to find a Neurologist to get further testing.

I made an appointment with my primary care doctor and the journey began. There was test after test, and doctor after doctor to find out what was going on. Still experiencing problems back and forth to the doctor I go. Until one day, I was sitting at my desk at work on lunch and I received a phone call from a doctor and she said, "Mr. Nelson, I am doctor so and so and

I am calling you to tell you that you have been diagnosed with Multiple Sclerosis." At that time, I knew nothing about Multiple Sclerosis, so I was told to read up on the disease and find a MS Support Group in my area. I was introduced to an MS Support Group at the VA Hospital in Washington, DC., by my mentor and great friend, Prophet George Carter.

During this time, I was going through a divorce and I realized that I had to keep going. I had been single for five years while diagnosed with Multiple Sclerosis. I met a young lady who had her own radio show called, "I Am Healed" blog talk radio," who later had me on her show. She also was diagnosed with Multiple Sclerosis. She was beautiful and a worship leader on a praise & worship team for a ministry in North Brunswick, New Jersey. After the interview, she joined The Huddle and led us in praise & worship every Sunday. She introduced me to blog talk radio, but we started talking on the phone more and more every day, seven days a week. From time to time, we Face timed and prayed together and watched TV shows while not realizing what God was doing. I believe that same year in October The Huddle had an event called The Gathering. The Gathering is an event when everyone from The Huddle meets for a three day MS event. That year we were meeting in Columbia, Maryland, at the Sheraton Hotel and I was excited because I finally got to see and meet her in person. Her name at the time was Christina Clemonts, the young lady I had built a relationship with through the phone. When she walked into the hotel, I felt like Adam- bone of my bone and flesh of my flesh.

I knew immediately that I wanted to pursue her and I didn't care that she was diagnosed with Multiple Sclerosis or she lived 3 hours away. It was like love at first sight. So as The Gathering ended and I had a few days to enjoy Christina in person, I knew that she had to go back home to New Jersey, I began to figure out how I would see her again. So November through December, we continued to serve together in ministry and we went back to calling and face timing. I believe because we built a relationship on the phone and saw her in person and because I missed her, I planned to take trips to New Jersey for a few days in January. We had so much fun that I decided to go up again in February for her birthday and Valentine's Day but, I bought something with me to let her know that I was serious about her, a ring. I popped the question. She said YES!!!!

CHRISTINA'S STORY:

Of course, I said yes! Why wouldn't I? I was diagnosed with MS in 2001. What a journey it's been! I was 27 years old. I just had my third child. A girl. MS came suddenly. Without warning. I woke up one morning and had no feeling in my feet. It was as if I had been sitting on my feet all night and they fell asleep, only I could not wake them up. I stood up, waiting for the blood to flow and the feeling to return, but it did not. That was the beginning of a 9-month journey for me. Blood work, MRI's, and second opinions led to hearing words I never expected to hear, "I'm sorry, but you have Multiple Sclerosis."

That was 20 years ago. I've had my share of relationships. Or maybe what I thought were relationships. Nothing ever went past boyfriend/girlfriend, and you couldn't tell I had MS by looking at me. I walked just fine, still wore my heels, etc. If you don't know, many people diagnosed eventually end up using some type of walking device, or walk with a limp. I didn't need anything until 2014. I had a relapse and needed a cane. It was then that I started to have all the insecurities rise up! Who would want me like this? I dated here and there, but honestly, no one wanted anything that was forever. I actually had men bold enough to tell me that my health issues were too much to handle.

Fast forward to the end of 2017. While on Facebook, this very attractive man sent me a friend request. That man was Erik Nelson. Yes ladies, I was checking him out! I had to see this man! I had a blog talk radio show called #IAmHealed, so I invited him to be a guest and the rest, as they say, is history. It pretty much went the way he stated. I admit I was smitten. The day we met in person for the first time, I was so nervous.

The 3-hour ride felt like 6. I had my daughter and another friend with me because hey, you never know, right? What will he say when he sees me walking up with my purple cane? (If I had to use one, it was going to be cute) The walk up to the hotel lobby was long and I finally walked in, and out of the corner of my eye, I saw him and let's just say, I was very glad I came. I can honestly say I knew he was the one for me.

Who knew that two people, both diagnosed with the same disease, would be perfect together? Did we question at first? Sure. I remember He asked me if I would ever date someone with MS? I actually never considered it till I met him. Do we have our struggles? Yes, but we have learned to work together. When he doesn't feel well, I'm there. When I'm not feeling my best, he's there—not knowing what God was doing behind the scenes. We were being set up in the most divine way. God would use this diagnosis to bring two like-minded people together to minister healing His way to people who needed to hear it most. So The Huddle and #IamHealed united.

I always wanted to marry someone and work side by side in ministry. I could see all the pieces coming together even before we started dating. I enjoyed helping and supporting him. Likewise, he helped and supported me with my ministry. I prayed concerning things like this. Not only did I want to work side by side, but I wanted a husband who would support me. He would give me ideas for my guests for my show and called in all the time. I eventually changed my talk show from #IamHealed to 'The Christina Nelson Show, Real People who Motivate, Inspire, and Heal.' I love working together. I love that he trusts me to develop ideas for The Huddle and still do my own thing. This was truly a divine connection.

ERIK'S STORY:

Due to the nature of MS, it was prophesied to me that the Lord was changing us from a support group to a ministry. We started having service every Sunday for people diagnosed with Multiple Sclerosis who were wheelchair bound, had mobility problems, and those who couldn't attend a physical church building. During that time, Christina sang on the praise & worship team at Grace Church of North Brunswick in New Jersey. So I would minister and she would lead worship. We became a great team. We were serving together in ministry.

The Huddle is a place that not only teaches biblical truths about healing but also empowers people to walk in healing and minister it to others. That's what 'The Huddle, A Place of Healing', is all about—providing a place where believers can apply God's Word and witness miraculous results! We believe that God wants us well.

So, we wanted to provide an atmosphere for people to come and jump into the Word, build up our faith and find out what God really says about healing. I believe that God has given us His Word to correct the situation. Speak the Word over the sickness until it disappears. No matter how long it will take, we have to keep declaring in faith that we are healed of the Lord. So, in 'The Huddle, A Place of Healing,' we believe that the WORD heals.

Our foundation is the Word of God. Our foundational Scripture is Psalm 107:20. "He sent his word, and healed us, and delivered us from destruction."

We believe God has given us His Word to correct the situation. Speak the Word over that sickness until it disappears. No matter how long it will take, keep declaring in faith that you are healed. So, the Word heals. We believe we conquer MS with the WORD of God.

People who attend The Huddle, A Place of Healing Place are taught God's Word concerning healing and how to apply it to their afflictions. Learning and applying the truth of the Word causes faith to increase and healing to manifest.

We currently have 258 members. We provide church every Sunday at 2 pm (EST) on YouTube and every Wednesday at noon (EST) on blog talk radio. You can also find us on Facebook and Instagram.

Our mission and purpose is to be a ministry where the sick will be instructed and taught through biblical teachings on how to receive their physical healing. 'The Huddle, A Place of Healing' is a Christ-centered ministry that teaches those who have illnesses and diseases what the Bible says about health, healing, and wholeness.

We want to encourage those looking to get married and who have been diagnosed with what doctors say can't be cured to trust God. He'll not only bring you what you want but what you need. There is someone out there who will have the ability to love you. They will walk in agreement with you (Amos 3:3). As a result, will take place will be a beautiful connection, ordained by the Father. Be open. You never know.

CHAPTER 10

Workplace

BY KIMBERLY MOSES

A LOT OF CHALLENGES ARISE with people on their jobs. When I was at my lowest, I experienced so many attacks. All I wanted to do was finish the shift and hurry back home to sleep away the depression. I would say, "Jesus" underneath my breath several times while working to get the strength I needed. I worked hard and didn't bother anyone, but that didn't stop my co-workers from not liking me.

There was an older Caucasian gentleman and he despised me. I could do nothing right in his sight. I was fast and he was slow. I was used to working with more patients at a faster pace because I was trained at a huge hospital. When I relocated to Colorado Springs, Colorado, the hospitals were 1/3 of what I was used to. I would complete my work an hour faster than all my co-workers. They couldn't believe it, so they would check behind me, looking for errors. When they found none, they looked for something to complain about. The only thing they could find was my headphones were on while I was working. I would have my headphones on, listening to worship music or

Joel Osteen to be encouraged. They didn't know that I would go to the bathroom on my lunch breaks and cry.

This man reported me to my supervisor, so I had to stop wearing headphones. I didn't tell my supervisors that this man doesn't complain when people bring their laptops to work. I knew that the enemy was using this man to prevent me from listening to the gospel.

At another hospital in town, I worked a night shift. There was an order they came from the printer for a tracheotomy patient. I didn't know the order had been printed and I was never trained to check the printer because the supervisor of the shift was supposed to tell me what to do. Anyways, they ended up blaming the missed order on me because I was an agency staff or travel therapist. I was asked not to come back to work at the hospital again even though I had worked there numerous times and helped the other therapists when I finished an hour before them. Again, I just wasn't like and didn't fit in. God truly set me apart.

There were numerous times where I experienced racism when I lived in Fayetteville, North Carolina. I wasn't promoted and didn't receive the critical care training that I needed to advance my career because of the color of my skin. I would always have to work at the rehab centers, which are maintenance care and simple treatments. I had to volunteer to work at a long acute care facility to get the necessary training I desired to be skilled in operating ventilators. God began to show me that when one door closes, He can provide another route.

I also dealt with lots of attitudes and combative patients. I remember praying for God to deliver me from anger. When I would go to work, I would have the worst nights because everyone came at me with rudeness and horrible attitudes. I got to the point of swallowing my pride and not evening responding. Once I changed my perspective and humbled myself, I was able to shake off the anger and submit more to God.

WISDOM

1. A light in darkness

Christians go through a lot on their jobs and deal with a lot of warfare because most don't go anywhere except work, home, restaurants, or the store. They have to experience warfare somewhere, especially when working around a bunch of sinners or unbelievers. We can't quit or transfer our jobs because of the attacks there. We must represent Christ and be a light in a dark place. If no one knows that you are saved, then that's a huge problem. We need to spread the gospel to all creatures. I used to read my Bible right in the open and it made people feel uncomfortable. However, when they needed prayer, they came to me. I was able to witness and draw them to Christ. Before God called me into full-time ministry, He had me laying hands and praying for the sick even though I wasn't a Chaplain.

2. Prayer

We need to pray and even fast sometimes before we go to the workplace, so we have peace that surpasses all understanding. Also, prayer can strengthen us to endure the demonic attacks and resist the enemy. Whenever I had to work with difficult people, I felt God with me helping me. It was reassuring that He would never leave me or forsake me. I knew that since I was feeling the presence of God, I had to watch my mouth and instead of getting an attitude back with a rude nurse, I would smile and say, "God bless you." We will win people over with the love of God and kindness. Don't give people something to talk about by being mean. They can never say, "I told you that they weren't a true Christian." Love them so they can't speak evil of your well-doing. Before God called me into full-time ministry, I would go into the chapel at the hospital and pray to get the strength I needed.

About The Authors

KIMBERLY MOSES STARTED OFF her ministry as Kimberly Hargraves. She is highly sought after as a prophetic voice, intercessor and prolific author. There is no doubt that she has a global mandate on her life to serve the nations of the world by spreading the Gospel of Jesus Christ. She has a quickly expanding worldwide healing and deliverance ministry. Kimberly Moses wears many hats to fulfill the call God has placed on her life as an entrepreneur over several businesses including her own personal brand Rejoice Essentials which promotes the Gospel of Jesus Christ.

She also serves as a life coach and mentor to many women. She is also the loving mother of two wonderful children. She is married to Tron. Kimberly has dedicated her life to the work of ministry and to serve others under the call God has placed over her life. Kimberly currently resides in South Carolina.

She is a very anointed woman of God who signs, miracles and wonders follow. The miraculous and incessant testimonies attributed to her ministry are incalculable, with many reporting physical and mental healing, financial breakthroughs, debt cancellations and other favorable outcomes. She is known across the globe as a servant who truly labors on behalf of God's people through intercession.

She is the author of The Following:

"Overcoming Difficult Life Experiences with Scriptures and Prayers"
"Overcoming Emotions with Prayers"
"Daily Prayers That Bring Changes"
"In Right Standing,"
"Obedience Is Key,"
"Prayers That Break The Yoke Of The Enemy: A Book Of Declarations,"
"Prayers That Demolish Demonic Strongholds: A Book Of Declarations,"
"Work Smarter. Not Harder. A Book Of Declarations For The Workforce,"
"Set The Captives Free: A Book Of Deliverance."
"Pray More Challenge"
"Walk By Faith: A Daily Devotional"
"Empowering The New Me: Fifty Tips To Becoming A Godly Woman"
"School of the Prophets: A Curriculum For Success"
"8 Keys To Accessing The Supernatural"
"Conquering The Mind: A Daily Devotional"
"Enhancing The Prophetic In You"
"The ABCs of The Prophetic: Prophetic Characteristics"
"Wisdom Is The Principal Thing: A Daily Devotional"
"It Cost Me Everything"

About The Authors

"The Making Of A Prophet: Women Walking in Prophetic Destiny"
"The Art of Meditation: A Daily Devotional"
"Warfare Strategies: Biblical Weapons"
"Becoming A Better You"
"I Almost Died"
"The Pastor's Secret: The D.L. Series"
"June Bug The Busy Bee: The Gamer"
"June Bug The Busy Bee: The Bully"
"The Weary Prophet: Providing Practical Steps For Restoration"
"The Insignificant Woman"
"The Foolish Woman: A Daily Devotional"
"June Bug The Busy Bee: Sibling Rivalry"

You can find more about Kimberly at
www.kimberlyhargraves.com

For Rejoice Essential Magazine, visit
www.rejoiceessential.com

For beauty and t-shirts, visit
www.rejoicingbeauty.com

Please write a review for my books on Amazon.com

Support this ministry:
Cashapp: $ProphetessKimberly
Paypal.me/remag
Venmo: Kimberly-Moses-19

All Things Relationships

Leslie Harvey

LESLIE HARVEY HAS COMMITTED her life to serving God. She is a dedicated active member of Word of Restoration International Church in Rosharon, Texas, serving in the Marriage ministry and Royal Priesthood children's ministry. She obtained her Bachelor's degree in Business Management from the University of Phoenix and owns Holly Gardens Young Adult home where she instructs young adults how to become productive in society. She is the co-owner of the Ministry of Directions, as a "Life Goal Advisor", Real Estate Investor (Tax Liens), Tax Consultant, and the author of Seed Time and Harvest. She is a certified Christian Counselor who loves to pray, intercede and assist others. This Los Angeles, California native currently resides in Houston, Texas, with her husband Irwin "Bug" Harvey; they have four adult children and four grandchildren.

Irwin Harvey

*I*RWIN HARVEY LOVES SERVING God and is a dedicated, active member of Word of Restoration International Church Apostle Charles Perry Jr. 1st Lady Charlette Perry, in Rosharon, Texas, serving in Marriage, Men's Ministry, and WORIC Security Team.

He has also acted as Chief Operating Officer Holly Gardens Young Adult Transitional Home, Co-owner of Directions Ministry, assisting individuals with achieving their Life Goals. He is a Real Estate Investor (Tax Liens). Currently, he retired from Michael DeBakey Veterans Medical Center, United States Army, and National Guard.

He is a Houston, Texas native who currently resides with his wife, Leslie Harvey. They have four adult children and four grandchildren.

Ms. Keima S. Sinclair

Ms. Keima S. Sinclair is a woman of faith, a Bible believer, and a servant of her Heavenly Father God through the Lord Jesus Christ. She delights in praising and worshipping, and dance. Ms. Sinclair is a mother, family-oriented, divorcee, entrepreneur, author, consultant, intermediary, and investor. In her lifetime, she worked as a cashier, hair preparer, and unlicensed stylist in a hair salon, telemarketer, administrator for a home improvement company, and a project assistant manager for a designer. With that, she's had a side hustle of styling hair on campus in school and in her neighborhood. She had other side hustles, such as selling new and like-new condition items, clothing, and vehicles online and with Tri-state TV advertising. She has great compassion for the elderly and takes the time to assist her elderly relatives.

Ms. Sinclair has an entrepreneurial spirit and owned a referral service business in NY and a day massage spa in Upper Montclair, NJ, in her early twenties.

As an author, Ms. Sinclair was encouraged to write her story about her past marital relationship to help young ladies and women and point them back to our Heavenly Father God through Jesus Christ, where our unconditional love, help, and true hope is in. She also shares her testimony concerning her children and without God, her favorable outcomes and victories would not have been possible. Ms. Sinclair's story testifies of God's goodness, grace, mercy, forgiveness, healing, being sustained and strengthened by the Lord to practice celibacy, being content and waiting patiently on Heavenly Father for His very best for her.

Ms. Sinclair is passionate about writing the miracles of her life so women and their children can learn to trust in God with all of their problems and challenges they will face in their lives. Also, for their salvation, deliverance, success, and blessings with their life fully dedicated to Father God and their walk in Christ Jesus. She desires the families to be equipped with Heavenly tools (the word of God and walking by faith, not by sight and putting Heavenly tools to practice) to be empowered to be victorious, overcomers and more than conquerors for their God-given calling and purpose through God who loves us unconditionally. Ms. Sinclair relishes in assisting and helping manage one of her daughter's song writing and singing gift/career.

EDUCATION

Keima was a nursing assistant and completed her certificate from Edison NJ Job Corps. She also completed a Human Resources Certificate Course at Cornell University, NY. She studied Metaphysical Science at the University of Sedona, AZ.

HOBBIES

Keima has conducted extensive research in natural extracts and steam distillation of plants, grasses, trees, leaves, fruit, nuts, and seeds. She Creates natural hair products, skincare for skin health, oral health care, ear health care, and massage with the benefits of promoting healing (pain relief and inflammation from the outside in, beautifying, anti-aging, and overall wellness). Many people have been blessed and helped with improvements concerning their conditions using Ms. K. Sinclair's custom formulas. Ms. K. Sinclair continues to work on her craft and plans to turn her hobby into a full-time business very soon.

Ms. Sinclair has traveled worldwide and has been to countries in Europe such as Amsterdam and Ukraine. She believed by faith she could take on this business and pleasurable opportunity to travel out of the country because she had small children and a newborn baby and did not have the financial means to travel abroad. She experienced God making a way and making this all possible.

Ms. K. Sinclair's other hobbies and interests are fishing, sightseeing of nature, horses, dolphins, turtles, goldfish as pets, watching Christian Comedy and Christian-based movies, including their films based on true events and true stories that are inspiring and edifying.

Ms. Keima S. Sinclair

FILM-TV

At 17, Ms. K. Sinclair was an extra in the film 'Private Parts'. She played the part as an extra being a college student in a Community College in the Bronx, NY, in the true story of Howard Stern.

In 2014, Ms. K. Sinclair appeared and participated in a demonstration on an episode of Doctor Oz at the ABC Studios in NYC, while Dr. Oz taught his audience and explained the benefits of Walnuts. Her younger sister accompanied her and was a part of the audience.

MINISTRY

Keima has been on missionary domestic trips: co-ministering, praying, and group singing for others in a senior citizen home in Paterson, New Jersey.

Ms. Sinclair enjoys Street ministry praying for people and sharing Gospel tracks to help their relationship with God the Father through Jesus Christ. She is ecstatic about getting her children involved in making homemade cooked meals during the holidays for the homeless and serving them with necessary items.

VOLUNTEER SERVICES

Keima has volunteered in General Hospital in Passaic, NJ. Ms. K. Sinclair has transported patients in the hospital in her early teenage years.

Ms. Sinclair helped and served the community by setting up and organizing food products, household items, and personal products to support the children and families who have lost their fathers due to violence. Shas has also served everyday people at her sister's organization, Faces of Fallen Fathers in the Great City of Paterson, NJ.

Ms. Sinclair can be contacted via email, Facebook, WhatsApp, or Telegram.
E: keeplookinguptothehills@gmail.com
FB: https://facebook.com/lookinguptothehills
WA /TG: (908) 899-1446

Erik Nelson & Christina Nelson

*P*ASTOR ERIK NELSON IS an ordained minister who is the President and founder of The Huddle, A Place of Healing, Inc. Christina E. Nelson is the host of The Christina Nelson Show. In this virtual talk show, she interviews real people with real testimonies. Her main goal is to motivate, inspire and heal. Together they teach those diagnosed with Multiple Sclerosis, Fibromyalgia, Lupus, Cancer, and other various illnesses.

They provide a virtual church service for people who are unable to attend a church physically. Pastor Erik and Christina have a passion and a heart to see the people of God healed. They encourage believers to know that God wants them well and He gave us His WORD to speak over that sickness until that sickness disappears.

They also wanted to provide an atmosphere for people to come and jump into the Word with Pastor Erik to find out what

God really says about Healing, with praise and worship lead by Christina. Once a month, Christina hosts a self-care Saturday for the ladies where they discuss various life issues. Erik and Christina Nelson currently reside in North Brunswick, New Jersey. Combined, they have three daughters, two sons, and five grandsons.

Gigi LaVonda Love

Gigi LaVonda Love is a mother of five adult children, two teenagers, and the Nana of ten Nana babies. She and her two teenagers reside in Jacksonville, Florida. Gigi was called to ministry as an Evangelist at the age of twenty years old while living in Langenselbold, Germany. She began pursuing mentorship and learning how to fast, pray, study God's word and learn how to be a young new wife and mother. After living in Germany for six years, she relocated back to her hometown of Glennville, Ga, and later moved to Leesville, La, where she lived for almost twenty-three years. While in Louisiana, she fulfilled her dream of becoming a nurse and attended Louisiana Technical College, Lamar Salter Campus, where she graduated in September 1999 as a Diploma Nurse and passed her nursing boards gaining the title of Licensed Practical Nurse. Gigi later attended Northwestern State University, where she graduated receiving her Associates Degree in General Studies. After moving to Jacksonville, Florida, she completed her studies, graduated, passed her nursing boards and gained a higher nursing title as a Registered Nurse. Gigi never gave up on ministry as it was her God-given purpose to minister God's word through preaching, teaching, and song. Gigi is an anointed praise and worship leader that sings and prophesy through song as the spirit leads.

While in Germany, Gigi was called the Evangelist that believed God working through her could save everybody, and she still does. Gigi began to operate in the gift of healing, word of wisdom, word of knowledge, and prophesy as she continued to be studious in the study of God's word and living a fasted and prayerful lifestyle.

Gigi has had several supernatural encounters with God through Holy Spirit and is also a dreamer. God has even told Gigi what her name is in the spirit as she has gone through many test and trails in her lifetime. Gigi loves to minister to all age categories and she has a special love for single mothers. God told Gigi that her mission is to give everyone what He gave her, His love. There is no coincidence that her last name is Love. God confirmed that it is prophetic and in line with her kingdom purpose.

Gigi has been anointed as an intercessor and has a heart of compassion for the widow, orphan, poor and homeless. Gigi desires to make a difference through the Holy Spirit's leading to see the prophetic fulfillment over her life to make a difference in Jacksonville, Florida, before moving on to her next assignment.

Gigi has been on the twelve-noon prayer call hosted by Prophetess Kimberly Moses ministry. She has had an article featured in the March 2021 publication of Rejoice Essential Magazine. Gigi has just written her first book collaboration with Dr. Zolisha Ware entitled Encountering Love and can be found on all social media platforms. She also launched Gigi Love Ministries in January of this year. You can find her on Facebook (LaVonda Gigi Love and Gigi Love Ministries), Twitter (eldergigilove49), IG (Gigi L Love), Clubhouse, and Facebook Messenger, Youtube (Gigi Love). Her email is gigiloveministries.com; P.O. Box 66175 Jacksonville, Florida 32208; 904-310-2839.

Index

1

1st Lady Charlette Perry, 103

A

abandonment, 34
ABC Studios, 107
abortion, 57
absent, 75, 76
abstain, 17
abundantly, 6, 33, 78, 81
abuse, 8, 9, 25, 62
access, 15, 30
accomplished, 39
accountability, 76
achievements, 18
acknowledge, 81
actions, 5, 23, 41, 46
Adam, 40, 89

Index

administrative assistants, 44
administrator, 104
admonition, 21
adorable, 65
adulterers, 70
adults, 30, 32, 57, 102
advance, 3, 64, 80, 96
advice, 18, 51, 64
affliction, 6
afflictions, 94
affordable, 30
afraid, 11, 36, 52, 63, 64, 74
aggravated, 31
alcohol, 60
allegations, 8
alone, 2, 25, 32, 43, 70
altar, 36, 38
analogy, 38
angels, 28
anger, 7, 51, 97
angry, 52, 67, 69, 73
anointed, 12, 20, 68, 99, 112
anointing, 17, 45, 47, 68, 77, 83
apartment, 41, 80
apologize, 62
Apostle Charles Perry Jr, 103
appointment, 88
argue, 20
argument, 8
armor-bearers, 46

army, 8
arrested, 8, 41
aspirations, 11
Associates Degree, 111
astonished, 76
astray, 67
atmosphere, 59, 93, 109
attack, 1, 2, 42, 87
attention, 33, 35, 43, 59
attitude, 57, 59, 68, 98
attitudes, 97
attracted, 4, 9
attractive, 91
audience, 107
aunts, 64
author, 99, 100, 102, 104, 105
authority, 24, 28, 44

B

baby, 8, 35, 57, 58, 106
Babylonians, 67
back burner, 48, 62
backslidden, 51
baggage, 83
bankrupt, 16
Barabbas, 46
bathroom, 96
beautiful, 74, 89, 94
beautifying, 106

Index

beauty, 13, 14, 101
beauty industry, 13
bedroom, 80
Bee, 101
behavior, 24, 25, 33
behaviors, 32, 56
beliefs, 84
believe, 5, 21, 30, 34, 51, 54, 59, 60, 69, 72, 89, 90, 93, 95
Believers
believers, 2
benefits, 13, 106, 107
betrayal, 8
Bible, 7, 10, 20, 27, 28, 31, 33, 50, 61, 63, 82, 84, 94, 97, 104
Biblical principles, 20, 23
bills, 11, 14
birthday, 10, 90
Bishop, 68
bitter, 52
bitterness, 60
blame, 7, 51
blessed, 13, 21, 24, 27, 30, 54, 55, 63, 75, 76, 77, 78, 79, 81, 82, 85, 106
blessings, 15, 17, 105
block, 1, 45
blog talk radio, 89, 91, 94
blood, 31, 90
bloodline, 80
Board of Education, 24
body, 1, 5, 28, 31, 80, 85, 87, 88
Body of Christ, 1, 2

bondservant, 48
book, 2, 39, 113
books, 12, 14, 101
boundaries, 3, 47
boyfriend, 6, 57, 63, 91
boys, 58
brain, 87
brand, 13, 99
breakup, 4, 7, 8
breakups, 3, 4, 8
breath, 95
breeding, 18
broken, 1, 2, 4, 5, 24, 42, 50, 83
brokenhearted, 5
brother, 1, 8, 53
buckler, 20
burden, 34, 83
business, 3, 12, 13, 14, 15, 19, 42, 43, 45, 58, 104, 106
businesses, 11, 14, 15, 16, 44, 99

C

calendar, 14
Cancer, 109
car, 65, 73
care, 1, 9, 12, 13, 17, 32, 46, 56, 57, 70, 83, 88, 90, 96, 106, 110
carnal, 19, 54, 85
cars, 9
cash, 14, 36
cashier, 104

Index

Caucasian, 95
cautious, 49
celibacy, 78, 105
ceremony, 65
chain of command, 22
challenges, 2, 17, 46, 95, 105
chaotic, 3, 20
chapel, 98
Chaplain, 97
character, 4, 15, 18, 19, 26, 32
chastised, 39
chemical imbalance, 33
children, 7, 8, 12, 14, 17, 18, 19, 20, 21, 22, 23, 24, 25, 26, 27, 28, 29, 30, 31, 32, 33, 34, 35, 41, 43, 44, 48, 59, 61, 69, 70, 71, 73, 75, 76, 77, 78, 79, 80, 82, 99, 102, 103, 105, 106, 107, 108, 111
Children, 17, 23, 25, 27, 28, 32, 44
choice, 53, 62, 67, 69, 84
Christ-centered ministry, 94
Christian Comedy, 106
Christian Counselor, 102
Christian movies, 30
Christian values, 84
Christian-based movies, 106
Christians, 15, 97
Christina Clemonts, 89
church, 7, 9, 10, 12, 20, 30, 35, 41, 61, 69, 78, 92, 94, 109
circumstances, 21, 32
City Hall, 74
clientele, 15

clients, 12
clothing, 104
Clubhouse, 113
clueless, 7, 66
Code of Ethics, 24
Colorado Springs, Colorado, 95
Columbia, 89
combative patients, 97
comfort, 26, 34, 65, 83
commissions, 31
commitment, 9, 56, 66
committed, 7, 8, 10, 31, 72, 85, 102
communicating, 7
communing, 22
community, 23, 108
compassion, 104, 112
compliments, 47
comprehend, 28
compromise, 13
concerns, 23, 24, 59, 78
concert, 41
confess, 18, 28
confession, 20
confidence, 10, 31
confirmation, 55
conflict, 31
conflicts, 2
confront, 23
confrontation, 22
congregation, 48

conquerors, 27, 71, 105
consequence, 17
consultant, 104
consulted, 68
conversation, 30, 53, 63, 71
conversations, 59, 61
converse, 22
convinced, 63
Cornell University, NY, 106
correction, 23, 28
corrupt, 18, 19, 56
corruption, 23
counseling, 22, 64, 68
countries, 10, 106
courageous, 74
court, 60
courthouse, 38
courting, 35, 37, 39
courtship, 3, 12, 57
cousin, 20, 58, 59, 63, 64, 65, 66
covetousness, 71
COVID-19, 13
co-worker, 10, 53
co-workers, 95
creation, 50
creativity, 29
crowd, 14, 43
crucify, 46
cry, 85, 96
crying, 7, 75

curse words, 14
cursed, 68, 73
cute, 65, 91

D

dad, 20, 57, 60, 69, 75, 76, 77, 78, 79
damage, 87
damaged, 5, 87
dark place, 13, 97
date, 10, 25, 37, 43, 53, 56, 57, 60, 78, 91
dating, 5, 7, 9, 10, 51, 52, 53, 92
daughter, 8, 41, 91, 105
death, 4, 6, 55, 70
debt, 99
deceived, 9, 54, 56
deception, 86
deceptions, 8
decision, 18, 19, 52, 55, 56, 63, 64, 67, 68
decisions, 4, 55, 67, 71
Declarations, 100
dedicated, 5, 56, 99, 102, 103, 105
defamation, 26
defend, 23
delegate, 42, 44
delight, 84
deliver, 55, 70, 72, 83, 97
deliverance, 20, 48, 68, 82, 99, 105
deliverer, 20
delivers, 77

Index

demonic attacks, 15, 98
demonized, 46
depart, 22, 44
depression, 69, 95
designer, 104
desire, 19, 34, 37, 73, 78, 81, 83
desires, 5, 18, 19, 28, 53, 58, 84, 105, 112
despair, 83
destination, 73
destiny, 2, 37, 61, 70
destroy, 15, 16, 38, 80, 81
destruction, 50, 70, 93
device, 91
devil, 7, 18, 23, 29, 44, 69, 80, 81
diagnosed, 87, 88, 89, 90, 91, 92, 94, 109
diagnosis, 88, 92
diamond ring, 74
difficult, 12, 15, 33, 55, 70, 98
dignity, 26
diligence, 22
diligently, 72
disagreement, 45
disappointment, 7, 8
disappointments, 20, 48, 52, 60
disaster, 86
discern, 47, 52, 67
discernment, 55
discipline, 20, 75, 76
disclaimer, 33
disconnected, 12

discouraged, 83
discouragements, 60
disease, 31, 60, 87, 89, 91
dishonored, 49
dismayed, 74
disobedience, 16
disrespectful, 18, 25, 28, 47, 57, 65
distress, 10
divine connection, 92
divine way, 92
divorce, 2, 5, 8, 9, 72, 73, 74, 89
divorcee, 19, 54, 78, 104
divorces, 44
dizziness, 32
doctor, 33, 88
Doctor Oz, 107
documents, 72
dolphins, 106
dominion, 86
donate, 13
door, 19, 21, 42, 57, 96
doors, 6, 11, 18
Doris, 53
double, 64
Dr. Zolisha Ware, 113
drama, 32
dream, 6, 16, 76, 111
dreams, 6, 19
drinking, 10, 60
dysfunction, 2

E

ear, 22, 106
earth, 17, 18, 53, 54, 70
eat, 38, 43
edifying, 30, 106
Edison NJ Job Corps, 105
editors, 44
educated, 24
effective, 3, 15, 28, 43
egos, 47
elated, 72
elevate, 47
embarrassed, 57
embarrassment, 51
embrace, 56
emergency, 47, 88
emotion, 9, 24
emotional, 8, 9, 60
emotions, 51, 52
encounter, 37, 40
Encountering Love, 113
encourage, 2, 42, 55, 67, 94, 109
encouraged, 1, 28, 29, 33, 75, 96, 105
endearment, 6
enemy, 1, 2, 7, 15, 16, 21, 24, 29, 40, 44, 46, 69, 96, 98
engaged, 6
entrepreneur, 99, 104
entrepreneurial spirit, 104

equally yoked, 68, 81, 84
equipped, 105
ER, 88
Erik Nelson, 91, 109
errors, 95
evaluations, 24
evangelist, 44, 68
Evangelist, 72, 111, 112
excellence, 12
excuse, 59
ex-girlfriends, 59
ex-husband, 5, 19, 41, 74
experiences, 59, 60
expertise, 15
expressions, 23
ex-wife, 9
eye-opener, 59
eyes, 17, 22, 63, 70, 78, 79, 80

F

Face timed, 89
Facebook, 91, 94, 108, 113
Faces of Fallen Fathers, 108
faith, 5, 20, 24, 32, 37, 72, 73, 82, 93, 94, 104, 105, 106
Faith, 100
faithful, 5, 21, 28, 55, 56, 61, 66, 74, 79, 80, 83
faithfulness, 31, 56
families, 1, 26, 41, 44, 53, 105, 108

Index

family, 3, 7, 9, 10, 14, 17, 19, 20, 21, 25, 30, 31, 32, 33, 41, 42, 43, 44, 46, 47, 58, 59, 61, 62, 63, 65, 69, 74, 80, 85, 104
fasted, 20, 112
father, 19, 22, 25, 34, 58, 61, 75, 76, 77
Father God, 26, 54, 55, 77, 79, 80, 81, 85, 105
fatherlessness, 32, 76
faultless, 86
faults, 18
favor, 9, 19, 25, 35, 82
favorable, 100, 105
Fayetteville, North Carolina, 96
fear, 13, 21, 26, 35, 36, 62, 67
February, 90
fiancé, 58, 59, 60, 61, 62, 63, 65, 66
Fibromyalgia, 109
fight, 20, 21, 23, 24, 25, 44, 72
financial breakthroughs, 99
financially, 8, 12
firm, 74
firstborn, 8
fishing, 106
flame, 26
flesh, 7, 19, 22, 40, 89
flirt, 43
Florida, 36, 111, 112, 113
flowers, 6
focus, 13, 54, 70
focused, 21, 35, 65, 70
food bank, 12
foods, 33

fooled, 55
foolery, 56
foolish, 20, 56, 61, 63, 64
fools, 67
forgive, 18, 23, 27, 31, 51, 52, 68
forgiven, 18, 51, 53
forgiveness, 19, 51, 52, 53, 55, 105
forgotten, 36
fornication, 63
forsaking, 1, 66
foundation, 5, 93
fragile, 45
friends, 30, 47
friendship, 5, 19
friendships, 1
fruit, 27, 78, 106
fruitful, 17
fruition, 73
fruits of the Spirit, 32
frustrated, 70, 75
frustrations, 48
full-time, 11, 73, 97, 98, 106
furious, 52, 80
future, 11, 55, 60, 70, 81, 83, 85
future husband, 81

G

Gathering, 89, 90
gazebo, 65

Index

generational, 20
generations, 34, 69, 80
Germany, 111, 112
gift, 17, 28, 31, 36, 82, 105, 112
gifts, 6, 26, 37, 46, 64, 77
Gigi Love Ministries, 113
girlfriend, 6, 57, 59, 63, 91
Glennville, Ga, 111
globe, 100
glory, 3, 18, 19, 51, 82, 86
God, 2, 3, 4, 5, 6, 7, 8, 9, 11, 12, 13, 14, 15, 16, 17, 18, 19, 20, 21, 22, 24, 25, 26, 27, 28, 29, 30, 31, 32, 33, 34, 35, 36, 37, 38, 39, 40, 42, 43, 45, 46, 47, 48, 50, 51, 53, 54, 55, 56, 58, 61, 62, 63, 64, 65, 66, 67, 68, 69, 70, 71, 72, 73, 74, 75, 76, 77, 78, 79, 80, 81, 82, 83, 84, 85, 86, 87, 88, 89, 92, 93, 94, 96, 97, 98, 99, 100, 102, 103, 104, 105, 106, 107, 109, 110, 111, 112
Godly man, 79
goldfish, 106
goodness, 25, 31, 105
gospel, 42, 45, 96, 97
Gospel music, 29
Gospel tracts, 77
gossip, 47
grace, 18, 31, 38, 39, 51, 55, 70, 84, 85, 105
Grace Church, 93
grammatical error, 15
grandfather, 85
grandmother, 17, 56, 57
grandparents, 17, 56
grandsons, 110

grasses, 106
grateful, 72
Great City, 108
grieve, 13, 21
grudges, 60
guidance, 10
guide, 28, 55, 84

H

hair preparer, 104
hair salon, 104
Hallelujah, 76, 84
hand, 21, 23, 51, 55, 69, 71, 88
happiness, 84
happy, 8, 36, 37, 57, 62, 63, 64
hardcore, 59
harvest, 21, 30
Harvey, 4, 6, 50, 102, 103
haters, 64
havoc, 7, 21
headache, 15
headphones, 95, 96
heal, 2, 5, 10, 31, 33, 70, 80, 83, 109
healing, 20, 34, 39, 52, 77, 83, 92, 93, 94, 99, 105, 106, 112
heals, 34, 55, 77, 86, 93
health, 2, 22, 25, 28, 31, 33, 66, 87, 91, 94, 106
hearken, 82
heart, 19, 22, 23, 26, 32, 33, 34, 36, 53, 58, 60, 61, 63, 69, 72, 73, 75, 81, 83, 85, 109, 112

Index

heartache, 20, 83
heartbreak, 36
hearts, 5, 27, 49, 84
Heaven, 17, 18, 21, 65, 85
Heavenly Father, 17, 18, 21, 22, 30, 54, 55, 60, 69, 71, 73, 75, 76, 78, 79, 81, 84, 104, 105
heels, 91
Hell, 63
help, 18, 20, 22, 25, 26, 27, 28, 30, 33, 39, 41, 42, 43, 46, 48, 57, 68, 69, 70, 73, 74, 80, 82, 84, 85, 87, 105, 107
helper, 20
hex, 68
High School education, 57
history, 31, 91
hobbies, 106
holiness, 6, 30
holy, 5, 30, 62, 80, 85
Holy Spirit, 13, 21, 38, 39, 51, 66, 73, 82, 85, 112
home, 6, 7, 8, 9, 12, 19, 20, 27, 29, 41, 44, 51, 56, 59, 68, 70, 90, 95, 97, 102, 104, 107
homeless, 112
honest, 20, 52
honey, 6
honeymoon, 46
honor, 6, 29, 47, 65, 73, 85
honorable, 84
honors, 82, 84
hope, 10, 26, 27, 28, 55, 73, 84, 105
Hope, 83
hoping, 65

horses, 106

hospital, 11, 31, 32, 95, 96, 98, 108

Hospital, 89, 108

hospitals, 11, 95

hostility, 50

hotel, 89, 91

house, 7, 17, 43, 44, 52, 53, 58, 59, 63, 74

household, 3, 67, 108

housewife, 19, 73

Houston, Texas, 102, 103

Howard Stern, 107

Hudson Valley, 76

humanity, 46

humble, 34, 38

humiliation, 7

hungry, 12, 31

hurt, 3, 5, 7, 10, 16, 18, 25, 36, 42, 46, 48, 60, 64, 71, 76

husband, 5, 6, 12, 36, 37, 41, 42, 45, 51, 65, 68, 69, 70, 72, 73, 74, 80, 81, 82, 83, 92, 102

hyssop, 39

I

I Am Healed, 89

idea, 5, 12, 24, 46, 52

ideas, 92

illness, 31

illnesses, 94, 109

image, 12

imagination, 85

Index

imagined, 55, 65, 78
impact, 3, 56
impossible, 3, 37, 72, 75
inappropriate situations, 61
income source, 14
individual, 15, 16
inexpensive, 84
infidelity, 4, 5
inflammation, 87, 106
influence, 2, 18, 29, 67, 76, 82
influenced, 12
inherited, 9
innocent, 24
inquired, 76
insecurities, 91
insight, 55, 82
instruct, 18, 27
instruction, 22, 57, 59, 61, 67
intentions, 23, 58, 78, 79
interceded, 20
intercession, 100
intercessory spiritual prayer warriors, 24
interests, 106
intermediary, 104
intervention, 24
interventions, 24
interview, 89
intimate, 4, 57, 64, 65
investor, 104
island, 1

isolate, 2

J

Jacksonville, 36, 111, 112, 113
Jacksonville, Florida, 111
jail, 41
jailed, 8
jailhouse, 41
January, 88, 90, 113
jealous, 47
Jesus Christ of Nazareth, 80
Jesus., 12, 13, 14, 31, 77, 105
job, 11, 31
journey, 12, 13, 37, 48, 55, 61, 87, 88, 90
joy, 27, 32, 84, 86
July, 88
Justice of Peace, 74

K

Keima, 17, 54, 104, 105, 106, 107, 108
key, 7
kill, 16, 33, 81
Kimberly Hargraves, 99
Kimberly Moses, 1, 11, 41, 45, 82, 95, 99, 112
Kingdom, 3, 13, 19, 40
knees, 22
knot, 65
knowledge, 62, 67, 112

L

labor, 43
ladies, 83, 91, 105, 110
lady, 45, 46, 89
Lamar Salter Campus, 111
language, 24
laptops, 96
laying hands, 97
leaders, 48, 49
leadership, 49
leaves, 33, 69, 106
legacy, 14, 56
legal counsel, 24, 26
legal matters, 9
Leslie, 4, 5, 10, 50, 51, 53, 102, 103
lesson, 49
letters, 22
LGBTQ+, 13
liar, 18
Licensed Practical Nurse, 111
lies, 8, 9, 60, 78
life coach, 99
Life Goal Advisor, 102
lifetime, 104, 112
limp, 91
lonely, 71, 83
long acute care facility, 96
long-term, 9

Lord, 7, 11, 15, 24, 27, 30, 31, 32, 33, 41, 48, 49, 60, 61, 62, 63, 65, 66, 67, 68, 70, 72, 74, 76, 78, 79, 80, 81, 82, 83, 84, 85, 92, 93, 104, 105

Los Angeles, 102

Louisiana Technical College, 111

love, 1, 4, 7, 13, 18, 20, 23, 25, 26, 27, 32, 33, 36, 46, 49, 53, 54, 55, 56, 57, 58, 61, 65, 69, 70, 74, 76, 77, 81, 83, 84, 85, 90, 92, 94, 98, 105, 112

loved, 7, 27, 28, 30, 36, 39, 43, 46, 52, 64, 71, 74

lowly, 34

lunch, 6, 23, 88, 96

Lupus, 109

lustful, 6, 79

lying, 52

M

Mable Esther B. Thomas, 56

mail, 66

maintenance care, 96

majesty, 86

malicious, 26

mankind, 55, 70

manuscript, 15

marijuana, 60

marriage, 2, 3, 5, 8, 9, 10, 17, 39, 43, 52, 54, 64, 65, 66, 67, 68, 69, 71, 72, 75, 76, 81, 82

marriages, 1, 9, 82

married, 5, 18, 53, 55, 56, 63, 64, 65, 66, 68, 69, 70, 72, 74, 82, 85, 87, 88, 94, 99

Index

marry, 7, 61, 63, 64, 80, 81, 84, 92
marvelous, 78
Maryland, 89
massage spa, 104
mate, 81, 84, 85
mean, 38, 98
media apps, 30
mediator, 15
medical doctor, 33
Medical doctor, 11
medicine, 11
Meditation, 101
meek, 34
melodies, 29
men, 13, 28, 30, 34, 38, 58, 67, 68, 75, 76, 78, 79, 85, 88, 91
mentees, 14, 47
mentored, 46
mentors, 75
mentorship, 111
mercy, 18, 25, 31, 51, 55, 78, 85, 105
message, 13, 47, 53
Metaphysical Science, 106
method, 28
military, 8, 10
mind, 14, 18, 19, 25, 28, 32, 35, 48, 61, 70, 71, 81, 83
minister, 6, 13, 42, 44, 45, 46, 64, 65, 66, 92, 93, 109, 111, 112
ministry, 3, 11, 13, 15, 30, 41, 43, 44, 45, 46, 47, 48, 50, 77, 80, 89, 90, 92, 93, 94, 97, 98, 99, 101, 102, 107, 111, 112
minor, 2
miracle, 26, 32, 76

miracles, 46, 77, 82, 99, 105
miraculous, 19, 82, 93, 99
misbehaved, 18
miserable, 3, 33, 66, 69
misjudge, 79
missionary, 107
missioned, 77
mistake, 19, 65, 85
mistreatment, 62
misunderstood, 71
mom, 17, 29, 57, 58, 59, 60, 62, 63, 64, 70, 79
money, 7, 9, 11, 12, 13, 14, 15, 19, 26, 73
monitor, 23
mood swings, 32
mother, 6, 8, 17, 23, 25, 28, 54, 56, 57, 58, 59, 60, 61, 63, 76, 99, 104, 111
Motherhood, 44
motions, 10
motives, 9, 13, 47, 78, 79
mouth, 59, 98
MS Support Group, 89
Multiple Sclerosis, 87, 88, 89, 90, 92, 109
multiply, 17
music, 29, 30, 95
myelin sheath, 87

N

National Guard, 103
nausea, 38

need, 1, 2, 9, 19, 20, 21, 22, 26, 34, 37, 39, 43, 44, 47, 48, 69, 77, 79, 80, 82, 91, 94, 97, 98
neglect, 39
neighborhood, 56, 74, 104
nephews, 30
nerve cells, 87
nerve damage, 87
nervous, 65, 87, 91
nervous system, 87
Neurologist, 88
New Jersey, 30, 89, 90, 93, 107, 110
New York, 30, 74
niche, 69
niece, 30
night shift, 96
nightmare, 24
North America, 13
North Brunswick, 89, 93, 110
North Jersey, 58, 76
Northwestern State University, 111
notarize, 72
nuggets, 37
nursing assistant, 105
nursing school, 37

O

obedience, 66, 77
obeying, 6, 28, 67
observation, 25

October, 89
offended, 1, 15, 36, 42, 45, 47
office, 11, 53
officer, 8, 9
omissions, 31
opportunities, 4, 37
optic nerve, 87
ordained, 94, 109
order, 53, 62, 96
orphan, 112
outcomes, 79, 100, 105
outfits, 2
overbearing, 15
overcome, 2
overcomer, 20
Overcoming, 100
overflow, 26

P

pagans, 6
pain, 7, 32, 51, 54, 71, 76, 106
painful, 69
pandemic, 15
paperwork, 66, 74
Parent Advocate Agency, 24
parents, 9, 19, 20, 21, 26, 41, 56, 60
park, 65, 66
partners, 1, 5
partying, 10

Index

Passaic, NJ, 108
passion, 6, 109
pastor, 20, 63
Pastor, 27, 28, 101, 109
Paterson, NJ, 108
path, 11, 55, 67, 75, 85, 86
patience, 17, 37, 61
peace, 15, 19, 21, 25, 27, 32, 70, 71, 76, 83, 84, 98
peaceful, 6, 23, 43
peers, 15, 22
perish, 71
permission, 57, 60
persuaded, 62
perversion, 13
pets, 106
phone calls, 6, 51
photo, 13
physical, 8, 9, 26, 44, 62, 79, 92, 94, 99
pillow, 68
Pillsbury buttermilk biscuits, 38
plans, 4, 19, 63, 106
planted, 2, 27
plants, 106
police, 9
policy, 25
poor, 55, 112
poorer, 66
popular, 14
pornographic stuff, 60
power, 5, 19, 20, 21, 32, 33, 67, 70, 78, 84, 86

powers of darkness, 68

praise, 26, 29, 51, 78, 80, 89, 92, 110, 112

pray, 2, 15, 17, 23, 24, 26, 28, 39, 40, 43, 44, 46, 49, 60, 66, 68, 77, 79, 83, 84, 98, 102, 111

prayed, 1, 6, 12, 20, 41, 58, 68, 79, 89, 92

prayer, 10, 11, 21, 22, 24, 28, 31, 33, 39, 44, 46, 47, 54, 66, 68, 69, 76, 77, 78, 79, 82, 83, 97, 98, 112

prayer groups, 21

prayer line, 11, 82

prayer requests, 21, 68

Prayers, 100

preacher, 44

preaching, 41, 111

pregnant, 35, 57, 60

President, 109

price, 47

prices, 14

pride, 34, 38, 47, 97

prideful, 45

Primary Care doctor, 88

printer, 96

priority, 19, 43

prison, 32

probation, 11

problem, 2, 14, 32, 97

procedures, 24

productive, 34, 76, 102

profit, 15

promise, 65, 72, 73, 83

promises, 5, 26, 28, 69, 70, 73

promote, 25, 46
prophecy, 11, 12, 36, 64
prophesied, 72, 76, 92
prophesy, 40, 112
prophesying, 12
prophet, 11
Prophet George Carter, 89
Prophetess, 82, 112
prophetic word, 36
proposal, 52
prosper, 2, 15, 87
protect, 15, 23, 36, 57
protector, 20, 75
provide, 14, 20, 26, 93, 94, 96, 109
provider, 6, 26, 75
prudent, 67, 84
psychology, 25
public school, 23
pulpit, 48
punished, 68
punishment, 17, 28, 56
purges, 39
purity, 85
purpose, 2, 3, 7, 37, 40, 54, 70, 88, 94, 105, 111, 112
purposeful, 57, 58
push-ups, 88

R

radio show, 89, 91

rap, 29
readable, 27
Real Estate Investor, 102, 103
rebellious, 44, 49
rebellious children, 44
rebuke, 2
rebuked, 39
recommendations, 25
reconcilable, 51
reconciliation, 3, 50, 53
red flags, 3
referral, 22, 104
refused, 67, 68, 80
Registered Nurse, 111
Registered Respiratory Therapist, 11
regret, 18
rehab centers, 96
rejected, 36, 59, 70
rejection, 61
Rejoice Essential Magazine, 12, 101
Rejoice Essential Publishing, 12
Rejoice Essentials, 99
rejoicing, 10
Rejoicing Beauty, 13
relationship, 4, 5, 7, 8, 9, 10, 28, 31, 34, 41, 43, 47, 48, 50, 51, 52, 53, 54, 55, 56, 58, 59, 60, 62, 65, 67, 68, 75, 77, 78, 79, 80, 83, 84, 89, 90, 105, 107
relationships, 1, 2, 3, 4, 8, 9, 18, 42, 55, 58, 59, 63, 67, 83, 90
relieved, 62, 72
religious, 25

remarry, 85
remorse, 9, 74
repented, 16, 36, 38
repenting, 7
reprimanded, 23, 24
reproof, 67
reputation, 23
rescue, 20, 75
research, 32, 33, 106
resistance, 61
responsible, 23, 34, 76
rest, 31, 34, 61, 76, 85, 91
restaurants, 97
restore, 5, 42, 69, 83, 85
restrict, 15
retaliating, 22
retaliation, 60
reunion, 50
revealing, 42, 79
reverence, 21, 77
rewrite, 29
rich, 15, 85
richer, 66
righteous, 21, 29, 79, 83
righteous living, 21
righteousness, 30, 39, 62, 85
rivers, 26
Rosharon, Texas, 102, 103
rude, 15, 98
rudeness, 97

Rumors, 26
Runaways, 32

S

sad, 1, 42, 46, 70
sadness, 5, 65, 74
salvation, 24, 60, 68, 69, 77, 83, 85, 105
sanctuary, 33
Satan, 24, 81
saved, 13, 97
scenes, 92
school, 22, 23, 25, 26, 28, 37, 56, 77, 104
School Counselor, 22
School dropouts, 32
school official, 23
school system, 23
schoolmate, 9
Scripture, 28, 63, 66, 83, 93
Scriptures, 31, 51, 68, 82, 100
season, 6, 47, 49, 72, 76, 80, 83
secret, 24, 39
security guards, 26
Sedona, AZ, 106
Seed Time and Harvest, 102
seeds, 30, 68, 106
self-pity, 18
self-pleasing, 71
self-will, 71
September, 111

Index

servant, 100, 104
serve, 48, 61, 90, 99
service, 12, 92, 104, 109
services, 12, 14, 15
sex, 14, 35, 60
sexual act, 5
sexual immorality, 85
sexual sin, 5, 85
sexually active, 5
Shalom, 40
shame, 7, 51
Sheraton Hotel, 89
shield, 20, 22, 57
shock, 57
shoes, 68
short- term, 9
shutdowns, 13
siblings, 57, 58
sick, 48, 83, 94, 97
sickness, 31, 66, 93, 109
signs, 7, 88, 99
sincere, 52, 57, 58
sing, 29
single, 28, 35, 56, 57, 83, 89, 112
sings, 112
sinners, 97
sister, 1, 8, 20, 41, 107, 108
situations, 21, 28, 79
sleep, 6, 64, 95
smile, 98

smiling, 64
smitten, 91
smoking cigarettes, 60
snow, 39
social media, 11, 37, 43, 46, 113
solution, 32
son, 18, 20, 22, 58, 61, 62, 66, 67
sons, 8, 75, 110
sorcery, 14, 68
sorrow, 15
sorry, 67, 72, 90
soul, 2, 5, 28, 44, 61, 72, 78, 81, 83, 87
South Carolina, 99
spinal cord, 87
spiritual connection, 2
spiritual warfare, 20
spouse, 43, 44, 55, 79
spouses, 2, 5, 8
standard, 2
steadfast, 5, 10
steal, 16, 81
steward, 13, 15, 30
store, 19, 55, 97
story, 17, 32, 40, 46, 51, 54, 70, 88, 90, 92, 105, 107
strategy, 1
streets, 10, 41
strength, 1, 10, 21, 26, 28, 29, 44, 55, 56, 60, 78, 95, 98
strengthened, 39, 83, 85, 105
strengthens, 13, 21, 71
stress, 15

stressful, 2
strong, 13, 23, 56, 74, 78, 82, 85
strongholds, 68
struggle, 11, 12, 15
struggles, 92
study, 24, 32, 61, 111, 112
submit, 2, 49, 81, 97
successful, 18
suffer, 6, 83
Sunday, 28, 89, 92, 94
sundown, 42
sunup, 42
Supernatural, 100
supernatural encounters, 112
supervisor, 96
supervisors, 96
supplementation, 33
support, 8, 20, 35, 43, 46, 48, 77, 82, 92, 108
surrender, 33, 60, 68
SUV, 41
sweetheart, 5

T

Tax Consultant, 102
teacher, 23, 75
teaching, 28, 30, 111
teachings, 20, 94
team, 89, 93
teas, 33

Teen pregnancies, 33
teenagers, 18, 111
Telegram, 108
telemarketer, 104
television, 69
temper, 19
temptations, 78
termination, 4
testimonies, 43, 82, 99, 109
testimony, 33, 42, 63, 105
testing, 25, 88
The Christina Nelson Show, 92, 109
The Huddle, 89, 92, 93, 94, 109
thirsty, 31
thoughts, 18, 80, 85
tired, 9, 12, 26, 35, 46, 48
title, 47, 111
toxic, 62
tracheotomy patient, 96
transition, 47
travel, 10, 19, 43, 96, 106
trees, 33, 106
trials, 11
tribulation, 21
Tri-state TV advertising, 104
Tron, 12, 99
true, 8, 13, 30, 53, 57, 58, 59, 76, 78, 98, 105, 106, 107
trust, 19, 22, 25, 26, 33, 55, 61, 79, 81, 85, 94, 105
trusted, 15, 31, 33
truth, 18, 27, 30, 42, 49, 70, 94

turtles, 106
Twitter, 113

U

unbelievers, 97
uncle, 25, 58, 65, 75
uncles, 75
uncomfortable, 97
unconditional, 17, 20, 105
understanding, 17, 20, 62, 66, 76, 98
unfairly, 24
unfairness, 23
unforgiveness, 60
unholy, 84
union, 64, 68
United States Army, 103
unjust, 26
unsuccessful, 4
Upper Montclair, NJ, 104
upset, 36, 41, 52, 59, 64

V

vagabond spirit, 49
Valentine's Day, 90
valid, 46
value, 14, 85
vehicle, 62
vengeance, 60

ventilators, 96
verbal, 8, 9, 62
victory, 32, 69, 73
violence, 8, 25, 32, 108
virtual talk show, 109
vision, 32, 65, 79
Vital Statistics, 66
vlogs, 45
vocal, 46
voice, 51, 53, 57, 66, 76, 99
voice messages, 51
voices, 18
volunteer, 96
voodoo, 68
vowed, 8, 66, 67
vows, 65, 66

W

warfare, 46, 97
warned, 12
waters, 26, 27, 66
way maker, 19
wealthy, 8
Wedding Anniversary, 42
weddings, 6
wedlock, 57
weeping, 72
WhatsApp, 108
wheelchair bound, 92

wholeness, 94

whoremongers, 70

widow, 112

wife, 8, 40, 44, 52, 63, 73, 80, 81, 82, 85, 103, 111

win, 35, 98

wisdom, 10, 21, 22, 25, 31, 32, 37, 43, 54, 55, 57, 62, 67, 77, 112

wise, 18, 28, 37, 61, 86

wise counsel, 18

witchcraft, 48, 68

witches, 49

witness, 8, 77, 93, 97

Woman, 100, 101

women, 9, 10, 14, 28, 34, 38, 41, 49, 68, 76, 99, 105

wonderful, 6, 41, 77, 99

wondering, 7, 67

wonders, 20, 99

Word of Restoration International Church, 102, 103

WORIC Security Team, 103

Workforce, 100

world, 10, 13, 17, 19, 41, 43, 69, 81, 85, 99

worldly ways, 51

worldwide, 99, 106

worship, 29, 68, 89, 93, 95, 110, 112

worth, 14, 34, 84

worthy, 34, 84

wounds, 5, 60, 83

wrong, 4, 6, 15, 18, 19, 23, 25, 26, 28, 35, 39, 40, 43, 49, 56, 57, 67, 79, 82, 88

Y

yoke, 34
YouTube, 94

www.ingramcontent.com/pod-product-compliance
Lightning Source LLC
Chambersburg PA
CBHW072016110526

44592CB00012B/1327